CREATIVE
FLORAL
arranging

CREATIVE
PUBLISHING
international

MINNETONKA, MINNESOTA

CONTENTS

President: Iain Macfarlane
Group Director, Book Development:
Zoe Graul

Created by: The Editors of
Creative Publishing international, Inc.
Printed on American paper by:
R. R. Donnelley & Sons Co.
10 9 8 7 6 5 4

FLORAL ARRANGING

Floral arrangements range from traditional table centerpieces to free-form wall swags to whimsical accessories. Whether made of fresh, silk, or dried materials, or a combination, they add color and help soften the lines of a room.

Arrangements can complement any decorating scheme. As accents in a room, arrangements can be enjoyed all year long or used as seasonal displays. Create a harvest basket for the kitchen, a floral centerpiece for the dining room, a wreath for the living room, or a garland for the bedroom.

When making a floral arrangement, consider where it will be placed when it is finished. Decide whether it will be seen from all sides or be placed against a wall or other surface. Select an arrangement style that suits your personal taste, and choose flowers and a container to complement the surrounding decorating scheme. Also consider the room environment; most living plants like humidity, sunshine,

and the lack of drafts; silks are the most suscept-ible to fading but are unaffected by humidity; dried naturals will last longer in less humid areas of your home.

Create floral accessories from leftover floral materials. Decorate picture frames, baskets, chandeliers, and wire forms, or make pomanders to hang in a window or fill a decorative basket. For added flair at the dining table, decorate a goblet, place card, or serving tray with flowers and foliage.

All information in this book has been tested; however, because skill levels and conditions vary, the publisher disclaims any liability for unsatisfactory results. Follow the manufacturer's instructions for tools and materials used to complete these projects. The publisher is not responsible for any injury or damage caused by the improper use of tools, materials, or information in this publication.

BASIC ARRANGEMENT FORMS

Floral arrangements generally follow a basic shape or geometric form. Arrangement forms range from triangular to linear to round. Several of the most common are shown here. The basic forms can be followed exactly, or they may be varied to suit your personal style preferences.

Fan arrangement *contains floral materials that radiate from a central point to form a semicircle.*

Oval arrangement *contains floral materials that outline and fill in either a horizontal or vertical oval shape.*

Crescent arrangement *contains floral materials that curve into a soft crescent shape.*

Horizontal arrangement *is usually low and follows a long horizontal line. The line may contain a slight arc.*

L-shape arrangement *forms a 90˚ angle at the base. The L shape may be reversed, if desired.*

Round arrangement *contains floral materials that outline and fill in the shape of a sphere. These arrangements are often used as centerpieces, because they look the same from all sides.*

Triangular arrangement *(right) contains floral materials that form a triangle. The shape of the triangle may vary from high and narrow to low and wide.*

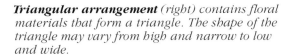

Vertical arrangement *is a tall, slender linear design.*

Parallel arrangement *contains two or more vertical groupings of floral materials, sometimes with space between them. The materials may be of varied or uniform heights.*

S-curve arrangement *contains floral materials that form a graceful S shape.*

FLORAL DESIGN

The basic elements of design are line, form, texture, and color. All these elements need to be considered to make an arrangement with good design that fits well into the room. You may choose to repeat elements from the room's decorating scheme in the arrangement. For example, a tall, vertical arrangement with a smooth ceramic vase is suitable for a room with tall, narrow windows and a dramatic decorating scheme.

For a floral arrangement, choose colors that complement or contrast with the colors of the room. To prevent the arrangement from blending in too much, use colors that are slightly lighter or darker than the room colors rather than an exact match.

Design principles such as balance and proportion are also important considerations. These principles are discussed on pages 10 and 11.

LINE

Line describes the directional movement in an arrangement. The line of an arrangement may be straight or curved.

FORM

Form describes the basic shape of an arrangement (pages 6 and 7). In controlled design, the floral materials stay within the boundaries of the shape. In free-form design, the materials fall outside the boundaries to add visual interest.

TEXTURE

Texture helps create the mood of a design. Smooth surfaces can look elegant; rough textures, more rustic. Consider the texture of both the floral materials and the container.

8

Single color can be used for the entire arrangement. Different shades of a color can be used to achieve contrast.

Neighboring colors on the color wheel harmonize, because they contain the same underlying color. For example, red-orange, red, and red-violet all contain the color red.

Evenly spaced colors on the color wheel can be combined for contrast.

Opposite colors on the color wheel can be combined to achieve strong contrast.

BALANCE

When an arrangement has good balance, the flowers are correctly positioned and secured in the container. This not only keeps the arrangement from falling over, but makes it visually pleasing as well. Visual balance is achieved when an arrangement looks balanced to the eye, as in the symmetrical and asymmetrical arrangements below.

Symmetrical balance is achieved by placing flowers in the container so, when an arrangement is divided down the center, it has two halves that look alike. Symmetrical designs are always visually balanced, because the placement of flowers on both sides is the same, or nearly the same.

Asymmetrical balance is achieved by placing flowers in the container so that when an arrangement is divided down the center, it has two halves that look different. However, the design is visually balanced, because the visual weight of both sides is the same.

VISUAL WEIGHT

When an arrangement is visually balanced, the visual weight of the flowers is distributed evenly. Visually, each flower in an arrangement has a certain amount of weight, or emphasis. This is partially determined by the flower's size and color. To achieve a balanced design, consider the information below as you position the flowers in an arrangement.

Size of a flower affects its visual weight. Large flowers have more visual weight than small flowers; however, several small flowers can be grouped together to achieve the visual weight of one large flower.

Color affects the visual weight of a flower. A light-colored flower has less visual weight than a dark-colored flower of the same size. It may take two or more light-colored flowers to give the visual weight of one dark flower.

Similarity of line, size, texture, and color makes the visual weight of one floral material equal to that of another. When similar materials are substituted for one another, the arrangement retains its visual balance.

HARMONY & CONTRAST

Harmony and contrast are used together for a unified floral arrangement that works well in its surroundings. Harmony is created when the arrangement uses elements that are similar to the surroundings, so the arrangement seems to belong where it is placed. Contrast is created when the arrangement uses elements that are different from the surroundings; this prevents the arrangement from blending into the room and gives it more impact.

Harmony exists when elements from the surroundings are repeated in the arrangement. For example, the soft colors in this arrangement blend with the room's color scheme. The shiny surface of the mirror and the glass container with marbles both have reflective qualities. And the white, dainty florets of hydrangea repeat the color and texture of the lace table runner.

Contrast exists when elements of the floral arrangement vary from the surroundings. For example, the majority of the colors in this arrangement are dark, to contrast with the light surroundings. The texture of the arrangement contrasts with the smooth finishes of the pillows and tabletop. The angular lines of the container contrast with the soft lines of the upholstery.

PROPORTION & SCALE

Proportion and scale are important considerations in making a floral arrangement that is suitable for its setting. For good proportion, the size and quantity of the flowers should relate to the size of the container. For correct scale, the arrangement is of a size appropriate for the location.

Proportion and scale relate the size and quantity of the floral materials to the container and relate the size of the arrangement to the setting. For example, the horizontal line of the arrangement works well on the rectangular table, and its height does not interfere with conversation. The arrangement is in correct scale with the goblets and dinnerware.

MAKING A BASIC ARRANGEMENT

In addition to the elements and principles of design, there are general guidelines for the placement of floral materials in an arrangement. The largest and darkest flowers in an arrangement are usually placed near the base of the design, and the smallest and lightest flowers are placed at the outer edges. In symmetrical arrangements, the floral materials are spaced evenly throughout; in asymmetrical arrangements, the floral materials are placed so the visual weight is distributed evenly throughout.

DOMINANT, SECONDARY, FILLER & LINE MATERIALS

Dominant materials are the largest materials in an arrangement. They are usually inserted after the line materials.

Secondary materials are smaller than the dominant materials and are used to finish shaping the form of the design. They are inserted after the dominant materials.

Filler materials usually consist of small flowers or foliage. Used to fill in any of the bare areas throughout the arrangement, the filler materials are the last items that are inserted.

Line materials are used to give line direction to the arrangement. Including flowers, foliage, or twigs, they are usually inserted first to establish the height and width of the arrangement.

HOW TO MAKE A BASIC ARRANGEMENT

1 Select floral materials, and determine the quantity needed by making a bouquet in hand. Check size and color relationships of materials, and determine if size of bouquet is appropriate for the container.

2 Select a basic form (pages 6 and 7), such as round, for the arrangement. Insert foam into container, and cover (page 23). Insert the line material into the foam to establish the height and the width of the selected form.

3 Insert the dominant flowers into arrangement, spacing them evenly and staying within the shape of the desired form.

4 Insert secondary flowers into arrangement, spacing them evenly and staying within the shape of the desired form.

5 Insert filler materials to fill in any bare areas of the desired form.

6 Add an element of interest, such as ivy, if desired, allowing the material to extend outside the basic form.

CONTAINERS

Containers are an integral part of a floral arrangement, often as important to the total design as the flowers themselves. When choosing a container, consider the color, texture, line direction, and size of the arrangement. Also consider where the arrangement will be placed so both the flowers and the container complement the surrounding decorating scheme.

The most common floral container is the vase. However, a variety of other containers can usually be found among kitchen cookware and serving pieces. Look around the kitchen for teapots, water pitchers, serving bowls, and other items made of glass, china, ceramic, or metal. All of these can make suitable containers for floral arrangements. An elegant serving bowl may be appropriate for a formal holiday arrangement, while an old teapot may be perfect for a dried arrangement in a country dining room. For garden-style arrangements, or for designs with a rustic look, select a basket, terra-cotta pot, or wooden box. Many containers can fit into any decorating scheme.

Country containers (right) *are often made of natural materials and include items such as thatched and reed baskets and terra-cotta pots. Old watering cans, wire baskets, and pottery pitchers also fit well into this decorating style.*

Contemporary containers (below) *have simple shapes and clean lines. Use glass or ceramic vases, terra-cotta pots, and metal containers with minimal detailing to accent contemporary arrangements and interiors.*

Traditional containers *are often elegant and refined. Metal containers, such as a silver teapot or a gold-plated candy dish, work well in traditional interiors. Many porcelain, cut-glass, and ceramic vases are also traditional in style.*

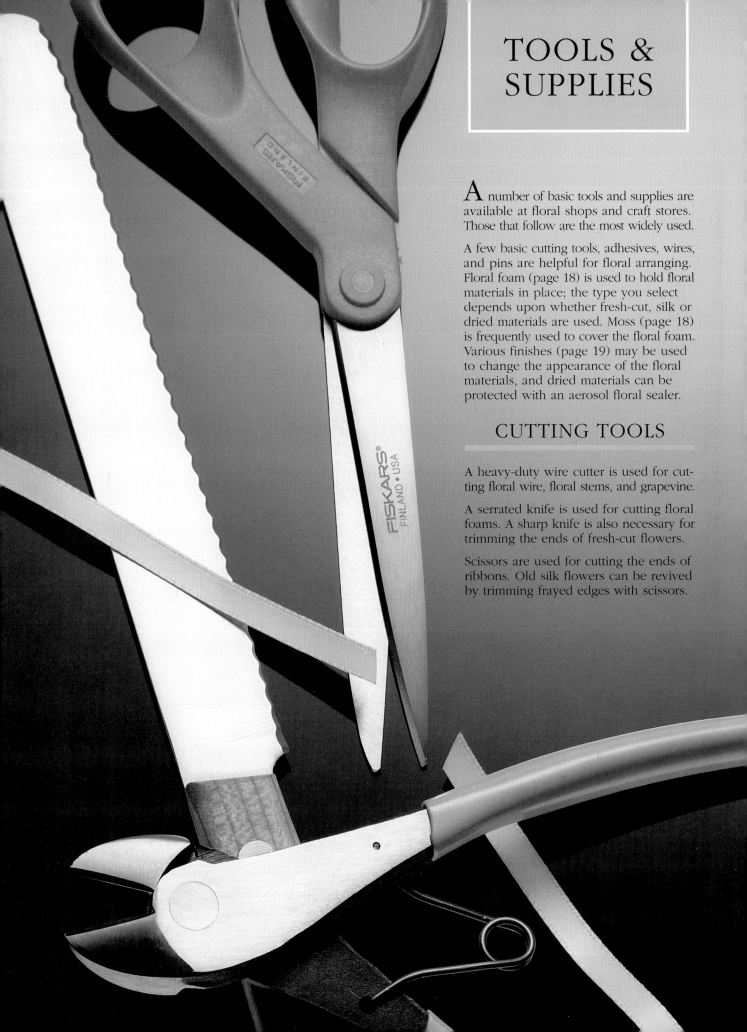

TOOLS & SUPPLIES

A number of basic tools and supplies are available at floral shops and craft stores. Those that follow are the most widely used.

A few basic cutting tools, adhesives, wires, and pins are helpful for floral arranging. Floral foam (page 18) is used to hold floral materials in place; the type you select depends upon whether fresh-cut, silk or dried materials are used. Moss (page 18) is frequently used to cover the floral foam. Various finishes (page 19) may be used to change the appearance of the floral materials, and dried materials can be protected with an aerosol floral sealer.

CUTTING TOOLS

A heavy-duty wire cutter is used for cutting floral wire, floral stems, and grapevine.

A serrated knife is used for cutting floral foams. A sharp knife is also necessary for trimming the ends of fresh-cut flowers.

Scissors are used for cutting the ends of ribbons. Old silk flowers can be revived by trimming frayed edges with scissors.

ADHESIVES

A glue gun and glue sticks **(a)** are used together to secure materials to a base. A glue stick is inserted into an electric glue gun, which melts it. Hot glue can be used to secure floral foam for dried arranging to the bottom of certain containers, such as baskets and terracotta pots. However, it causes floral Styrofoam (page 18) to melt.

Floral tape **(b)** is a narrow tape on a roll and is usually green in color. Made from wax and paper, it is used to cover wires and floral stems.

Thick white craft glue **(c)** can be used for securing flower petals and leaves to floral Styrofoam or other bases.

Floral adhesive clay **(d)** is used for securing floral Styrofoam for silk arranging to a base. It will not adhere to floral foam for dried arranging.

WIRES & PINS

Floral pins **(a)**, sometimes called U or S pins, are used to secure moss or other floral materials to foam or straw bases.

Stem wire **(b)** is used to extend the length of floral stems and to bind floral materials together. It is sized by gauge, ranging from 16 to 28. The smaller the number, the thicker the wire.

Floral picks **(c)** are used to extend the length of floral stems and add stems to artificial fruit (page 24).

Paddle floral wire **(d)**, usually thin to medium in gauge, is wrapped around a paddle. It is used when long lengths of wire are necessary.

Anchor pins **(e)** are small plastic holders, used to hold floral foam in place. Anchor pins are secured to the container using floral adhesive clay.

MOSSES

Sheet moss **(a)** comes in dried sheets and is used for covering the floral foam in arrangements. It can also be used decoratively to cover a container or wreath base.

Spanish moss **(b)** is used to cover the foam in arrangements. It can be secured to the foam with floral pins.

Reindeer moss **(c)** has a spongy texture. It is added to a finished arrangement for visual interest.

Excelsior **(d)** is added to an arrangement for texture and for visual interest. These curled wood shavings are available bleached or unbleached.

FLORAL FOAMS

Floral Styrofoam® for silk arranging **(a)** is available in sheet form, in green or white, and is used to hold and stabilize floral materials in a silk arrangement. It is available in preshaped forms, such as balls, cones, and eggs, which can be used for making topiaries or pomanders. It is also available in various wreath forms.

Floral foam for dried arranging **(b)** is grayish brown and usually comes in a block. It is used to hold and stabilize dried floral materials in an arrangement.

FINISHES

Aerosol paint (a) can be applied to pinecones, foliage, branches, and pods to change their colors or to add a metallic finish.

Acrylic paint (b) can be brushed on leaves, flower petals, and dried or artificial fruit to add visual interest and color contrast.

Aerosol floral sealer (c) can be applied to dried materials to help prevent shattering.

Wax-based paint (d) can be rubbed onto floral materials to give a metallic finish.

WORK AREA & STORAGE

Although dried and silk flowers can be arranged almost anywhere, kitchen counters and tables usually provide good work areas. Work near an electrical outlet if using a glue gun. Because it can be messy to work with moss and dried materials, cover the work surface with newspaper, and keep a large trash can nearby. For convenience, use a sheet of Styrofoam® to hold floral pins, picks, anchor pins, and stem wire.

When working on an arrangement, place it so it will be arranged at the same height from which it will be viewed when displayed. Or, during arranging, place the arrangement in its final location occasionally, to check the placement of the floral materials. When working on larger projects, such as garlands, allow plenty of room, so the entire project fits on the work surface.

Store silk floral materials upright; they can become flattened or wrinkled if they are stored flat. Keep them out of direct sunlight to prevent fading. Store dried floral materials by hanging them upside down from hooks or by laying them on crumpled tissue paper and storing them in cardboard boxes. To prevent dried materials from fading and molding, keep them in a location that is dark, dry, and well ventilated.

20

TIPS FOR THE WORK AREA

Pegboard can be convenient for holding a wall swag while you arrange it. This allows you to see how the swag will look when it is displayed. The pegboard is also helpful for keeping floral tape, ribbons, and cutting tools within easy reach.

Cardboard box is used to elevate a centerpiece to the same height as its final display location. This makes it easier to achieve balance and even distribution of floral materials.

TIPS FOR STORAGE

Silk materials are easily stored by placing floral Styrofoam in the bottom of a cardboard box and inserting flowers upright into the foam. Cover the box with dark plastic to prevent the materials from fading.

Dried floral materials are stored by hanging them in bunches from a dowel. Flower heads are stored in a cardboard box and cushioned with tissue paper. A small amount of silica gel (page 83) may be placed in the bottom of the box, to absorb any moisture. Flat floral materials, such as mosses and leaves, are stored by laying them on crumpled newspaper in a cardboard box.

PREPARING FLORAL FOAM

Floral foam for silk and dried arrangements can be secured to the container in several ways, depending on the type of foam and the type of container being used.

Floral foam is used as a holding device to secure and stabilize flowers in an arrangement. Floral Styrofoam® is sturdy foam designed for use with silk and artificial floral materials; it comes in a variety of shapes and is usually green or white. Dried floral materials are fragile and therefore require a soft floral foam to prevent stems from breaking when they are inserted. Floral foam appropriate for dried arranging is grayish brown and usually comes in block form.

Floral foam can be secured to containers in several ways, depending on the type of foam and the container being used. The simplest method is to wedge the foam tightly into the container to prevent the foam from shifting.

Floral foam for dried arranging can be secured to many containers, using hot glue. Avoid gluing foam pieces together, because the glued area hardens, making it difficult to insert the stems, and forcing stems could cause breakage. Floral adhesive clay does not stick to floral foam for dried arranging. In order to use floral

foam for dried arranging with floral adhesive clay, you must secure an anchor pin to the bottom of the container, using floral adhesive clay. Then insert the floral foam into the container over the anchor pin.

Floral Styrofoam for silk arranging can be secured to most containers using floral adhesive clay. Hot glue is usually avoided, because it melts Styrofoam; when hot glue is used, allow the glued surface to cool slightly before placing it in direct contact with the Styrofoam.

The height of the foam in an arrangement depends on whether the arrangement is vertical or horizontal, and whether the floral stems are flexible. For vertical floral arrangements, the foam usually falls ½" to ¾" (1.3 to 2 cm) below the rim of the container. For horizontal or draping arrangements, the foam is usually even with or extends above the rim. Less flexible stems require foam that extends to about 1" (2.5 cm) above the container. This makes it easier to position floral materials outward or downward near the rim.

PREPARING FLORAL FOAM FOR NONGLASS CONTAINERS

1 Vertical floral arrangement. Select appropriate type of floral foam for a dried or silk arrangement. Cut foam, using knife, so it fits container snugly and is ½" to ¾" (1.3 to 2 cm) below rim; cut and insert wedges of foam as necessary.

2 Cover foam lightly with moss, securing it with floral pins, if necessary.

1 Horizontal or draping floral arrangement. Select appropriate type of floral foam for a dried or silk arrangement. Cut the foam, using knife, so it fits the container snugly and is even with or extends about 1" (2.5 cm) above container, depending on flexibility of the floral stems. Round off the top edges of foam, if necessary, to prevent foam from showing in finished arrangement.

2 Cover foam lightly with moss, securing it with floral pins, if necessary.

PREPARING FLORAL FOAM FOR GLASS CONTAINERS

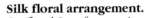

Silk floral arrangement. Cut floral Styrofoam so it can be inserted into center of the container with space around all sides. Apply floral adhesive clay to bottom of foam; secure to bottom of container. Fill surrounding area with potpourri, marbles, small pinecones, or other desired material.

Dried floral arrangement. Cut block of floral foam so it can be inserted into the center of container with space around all sides. Apply floral adhesive clay to the bottom of anchor pin; secure to the bottom of glass container. Press the foam firmly onto prongs of anchor pin. Fill surrounding area with marbles, potpourri, small pinecones, or other desired material.

Add wire stems **(a)** to artificial fruits and vegetables by inserting heavy stem wire into fruit and securing with hot glue; conceal the wire with floral tape, or add floral picks **(b)** to fruits and vegetables by making a small hole in fruit with an awl; insert a pick into hole, securing it with hot glue.

Gild silk and dried materials such as leaves, artichokes, and cones with metallic aerosol paint.

Add stems to pinecones by wrapping stem wire around bottom layers of the pinecone, twisting to secure. Wrap wire with floral tape before securing to pinecones, if desired.

Bend and shape the leaves and petals of artificial floral materials for a more natural appearance.

Rub gold wax-based paint onto firm floral materials, such as pomegranates, to add highlights.

Brush acrylic paints onto silk floral petals or leaves to accent them or to give dimension to the materials.

Add flexibility to dried floral stems by placing stem wire against natural stem and wrapping the two together with floral tape.

Extend lengths of silk floral stems by placing stem wire against stem; secure together, using floral tape **(a),** or wire the stems to wooden picks **(b).**

Clean dried floral materials and hand-wrapped silk materials by using a hair dryer to blow away dust.

Highlight twigs or other floral materials with glitter, frost, or aerosol paint.

Glue wire stems to dried flower heads, using a hot glue gun. Conceal wire by wrapping it with floral tape.

Protect fragile dried floral materials from shattering by spraying them with an aerosol floral sealer.

Clean floral materials with plastic stems by submerging them in water.

Separate bunches of dried flowers by holding them over steam for 1 to 2 minutes; remove from steam, and pull stems apart gently.

25

Fresh-cut
& Living
Florals

DECORATING WITH
FRESH FLOWERS

Fresh flowers add a luxurious quality to the home. Hand-picked from your own garden or purchased from the florist, fresh flowers can be easily arranged, following a few simple tips. They can be displayed as candlestick arrangements (page 196) or table wreaths (page 96) and in many other creative ways (page 192).

The long-lasting flowers listed below are excellent choices for table arrangements at dinner parties, because they can be arranged ahead of time. If the arrangement will be made in advance, select compact blossoms.

Keep fresh-cut flowers out of direct sunlight and drafts, add cut-flower food to the water, and add fresh water daily. Mist the blossoms in the arrangement to increase the freshness time. Do not, however, mist the blossoms of orchids and succulents, because misting them causes brown spots.

TIPS FOR USING FRESH FLOWERS

Cut stems of roses under water and on the diagonal, about 2" (5 cm) from the end, using a sharp knife. When stems are not cut under water, air bubbles form at the ends of stems, preventing water from rising up the stems.

Hammer the stems of woody plants, such as yarrow, forsythia, and blossoming tree branches, for 1½" to 2" (3.8 to 5 cm), to increase water absorption; for sunflowers, hammer stems lightly.

Cut the stems of most fresh flowers on the diagonal, using sharp knife, to increase water absorption. Snap stems of chrysanthemums.

LONG-LASTING FRESH FLOWERS

VARIETY	AVAILABLE COLORS	LASTING TIME
ALLIUM	Purple and white	10 to 12 days
ALSTROEMERIA	Many colors	8 to 10 days
ASTER	Purple and white	8 to 10 days
BABY'S BREATH	White	7 to 14 days
CARNATION	Many colors	7 to 14 days
CHRYSANTHEMUM	Many colors	10 to 12 days
CORNFLOWER	Blue and pink	8 to 10 days
FORSYTHIA	Yellow	12 to 14 days
FREESIA	Yellow, pink, purple, and white	5 to 7 days
FRUIT-TREE BLOSSOM	Many colors	10 to 14 days
GINGERROOT HELICONIA	Red and pink	8 to 10 days
HEATHER	Purple and mauve	10 to 14 days
LIATRIS	Purple and white	7 to 10 days
LILY	Many colors	7 to 10 days
ORCHIDS	Many colors	5 to 10 days
ROSE	Many colors	5 to 7 days
STAR-OF-BETHLEHEM	White	10 to 14 days
STATICE	Many colors	14 to 21 days
SUNFLOWER	Yellow with brown	14 to 21 days
YARROW	White and yellow	10 to 14 days

Remove pollen from lilies by pulling out the stamens. Falling pollen discolors the petals of the lilies and stains table linens and clothing.

FRESH FLORAL
ARRANGEMENTS

Buffets and centerpieces are typical focal points for fresh floral arrangements, especially when entertaining. A centerpiece on the dining table is usually short in height so it does not interfere with conversation, and because it is seen from all sides, it is usually symmetrical in shape. A buffet arrangement is designed to be placed against a wall, so it is often three-sided. It can be taller for more impact.

To make an arrangement, use long-lasting flowers such as those on pages 29 and 32. Sprigs of greenery, such as Scotch pine, spruce, or juniper are appropriate additions for winter arrangements. For a festive holiday look, embellish the arrangement with canella berries, decorative pods, pepper berries, pinecones, feathers, or seeded eucalyptus.

A fresh arrangement can be displayed in any container that holds water. For baskets, terra-cotta pots, or metal pots, use a plastic waterproof container as a liner.

Fresh flowers can be held in the arrangement by either of two methods, depending on the container selected. For glass containers, the flowers are held in place by making a grid over the mouth of the container with clear waterproof tape. For nonglass containers, the flowers are held in place by inserting them into floral foam designed for fresh flowers.

MATERIALS

- Flowers in three sizes.
- Sprigs of two or more varieties of greenery.
- Tall linear floral material, such as gilded devil's claw heliconia, curly willow, or branches, for the buffet arrangement.
- Gilded pods, berries, or twigs, for the centerpiece.
- Floral foam, designed for fresh flowers, for use with nonglass containers.
- Clear waterproof floral tape.
- Sharp knife.

Centerpiece (above) combines chrysanthemums, roses, ornithogalum, leatherleaf, seeded eucalyptus, lotus pods, and cedar. Buffet arrangement (opposite) uses mums, lilies, leptosporum, roses, gilded devil's claw heliconia, leatherleaf, and seeded eucalyptus to create a dramatic display.

Carnations

Orchid

Yarrow

Lily

Chrysanthemums

Ornithogalum

Heather

Alstroemeria

Roses

Stock

Leptosporum

Flowers shown above can be used to make long-lasting arrangements. Other options are included in the chart on page 29.

HOW TO PREPARE THE CONTAINER

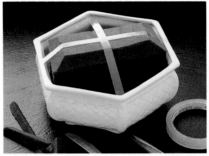

1 Nonglass containers. Soak the floral foam in water containing cut-flower food for at least 20 minutes.

2 Cut foam, using a knife, so it fits the container and extends about 1" (2.5 cm) above rim. Round off the upper edges of foam, if necessary, to prevent foam from showing in the finished arrangement. Secure with clear waterproof tape. Add water.

Tall containers. Make a grid over the mouth of container, using clear waterproof floral tape.

HOW TO MAKE A FRESH FLORAL BUFFET ARRANGEMENT

1 Prepare container (above). Insert first variety of greenery into container, placing taller stems into center near back and shorter stems at sides and front.

2 Insert remaining varieties of greenery. Insert tall linear materials into container, spacing them evenly.

3 Insert largest flowers into the arrangement, one variety at a time, spacing them evenly throughout to keep arrangement balanced on three sides.

4 Insert second largest flowers into arrangement, spacing evenly. Insert the smaller flowers into the arrangement to fill any bare areas. Mist arrangement lightly with water.

HOW TO MAKE A FRESH FLORAL CENTERPIECE

1 Prepare the container (opposite). Cut sprigs of greenery to lengths of 5" to 8" (12.5 to 20.5 cm); trim away any stems near ends of sprigs.

2 Insert sprigs of greenery into the container, placing longer sprigs around the outside and shorter sprigs near the center.

3 Insert the largest flowers into the container, placing one stem in the center and several stems on each side to establish the height and width of the arrangement. Insert remaining large flowers, spacing evenly.

4 Insert the second largest flowers into the arrangement, one variety at a time, spacing evenly, so the arrangement appears balanced from all sides.

5 Insert additional sprigs of greenery as necessary to fill in any bare areas. Insert gilded pods, twigs, or berries, if desired, for further embellishment. Mist arrangement lightly with water.

CONTAINER GARDENS & TERRARIUMS

Live plants add softness to predominantly hard-surfaced rooms, such as the kitchen and bath. For an ever-changing room accent, they can be grown in a container garden or terrarium. Plants can thrive, provided they are carefully selected according to the room's environment. Refer to the chart on page 36 for recommended varieties. Kitchens and bathrooms provide more humidity than other rooms in the house, which is a healthier environment for many plants. Many bathrooms, however, are low in light, limiting the selection of suitable plants. If the bathroom has insufficient light, make two container gardens or terrariums, rotating them periodically from a well-lit room to the bathroom.

CONTAINER GARDENS

Container gardens are essentially a grouping of plants growing together in a single container, such as a ceramic dish or a basket. A European dish garden has a blooming plant added to the grouping. For a pleasing variety, select plants of varying heights and include one or more plants that vine, such as ivy and philodendron. Choose plants that complement each other, such as spiky plants mixed with bushy plants, and dark green plants mixed with variegated ones.

African violets are a good choice for European dish gardens, because they bloom for about six weeks and like humidity. Although they need high light until they bloom, they can then be placed in a room with less light. Other blooming plants are included on the chart on page 36.

Select a container at least 3" (7.5 cm) deep. If the container has drainage holes, keep a saucer under it to catch the excess water; if it does not have drainage holes, prepare the container with charcoal and rocks (page 36). A basket may be used for a container garden, provided it has a plastic liner.

Water the container garden as necessary to keep the soil moist to the touch, using either spring water or hard water; soft water should not be used, because it contains salt. For healthy plant growth, fertilize the plants, using a fertilizer recommended by the greenhouse.

TERRARIUMS

Terrariums thrive on moisture. The plants are nestled in a glass goldfish bowl to create a greenhouse environment. Plant a terrarium as you would a container garden, using charcoal and rock in the bottom of the bowl. As an additional design element, decorative rocks, coral, shells, bark, or small twigs may be added to the terrarium.

Select a variety of slow-growing plants that will not quickly outgrow the confined space. Popular varieties for terrariums include peperomia, baby's tears, Venus flytrap, podocarpus, and maidenhair fern. Small palms and orchids may also be used, although they tend to grow large. Select the varieties that are suitable for the light level in the room (page 36). Care for a terrarium by watering and fertilizing it as you would a container garden, above.

PLANT VARIETIES SUITABLE FOR CONTAINER GARDENS & TERRARIUMS

LIGHT CONDITIONS	CONTAINER GARDENS	TERRARIUMS
LOW LIGHT	Cast-iron plant; China doll; Chinese evergreen; Dallas fern; maidenhair fern; moss; Neanthe Bella palm; all varieties of philodendron; podocarpus; silver queen. Blooming plants include anthurium and spathiphyllum, also known as peace plant. African violets may be placed in low light once they are in bloom.	Baby's tears; small bamboo palm; moss; all varieties of peperomia; podocarpus; maidenhair fern.
MEDIUM LIGHT	Asparagus fern; bamboo palm; birdsnest fern; Bolivian Jew; Boston fern; button fern; all varieties of dracaena; fluffy ruffles fern; Hawaiian ti; nephthytis; oak leaf ivy; all varieites of peperomia; podocarpus; pothos; prayer plant; ribbon plant; spider plant; Swedish ivy; wandering Jew; white fittonia. African violets may be placed in medium light once they are in bloom.	Baby's tears; small bamboo palm; all varieties of peperomia; podocarpus; Venus flytrap.
HIGH LIGHT	Aloe; Areca palm; croton; dwarf pineapple, most varieites of ivy; ming Aralia. Blooming plants include African violet; bromeliad; cyclamen; orchid.	Venus flytrap; orchid.

HOW TO MAKE A CONTAINER GARDEN OR TERRARIUM

MATERIALS

- Several plant varieties in varying heights, suitable for humidity and light level of the room.
- Container at least 3" (7.5 cm) deep; clear glass goldfish bowl, for terrarium.
- Crushed charcoal and river rocks or marble rocks, for use in terrarium or any container without drainage holes.
- Potting soil.
- Moss, optional.
- Embellishments, such as seashells, coral, decorative rocks, bark, or twigs, for terrarium.

1 Containers with drainage holes. Place a piece of broken pottery so it arches over drainage hole; this helps prevent hole from becoming clogged with soil. Add 1" to 2" (2.5 to 5 cm) layer of rocks, gravel, pottery shards, or Styrofoam® beads.

1 Containers without drainage holes. Pour ½" (1.3 cm) layer of crushed charcoal in the bottom of container, then ½" (1.3 cm) layer of river rocks or of marble rocks. Pour 1" (2.5 cm) layer of potting soil on top of the rocks.

2 Test-fit the plants while they are still in their containers to determine desired arrangement and spacing. Remove plants carefully from original pots, holding plant upside down and gently pulling it from container.

36

4 Arrange plants, nestling them together and surrounding them with potting soil. Plant taller plants toward the back and shorter ones toward the front. Root balls should be ½" to 1" (1.3 to 2.5 cm) below the rim of container. Take care not to overcrowd the plants, to allow room for the roots to grow.

5 Fill in remaining space with potting soil. Water the garden until the potting soil is moderately saturated.

6 Cover soil with moss, if desired. Use paintbrush to brush away any soil on leaves or container. Check the moisture level in 24 hours.

European dish garden. Follow steps 1 to 6, opposite, except do not remove blooming plant from its original pot; nestle the potted plant with other plants in the garden. When blooming has stopped, the plant may be replaced with a fresh blooming plant.

Terrarium. Follow steps 1 to 6, opposite, using clear glass goldfish bowl as the container. After plants are in place, add desired design elements, such as seashells, coral, decorative rocks, bark, or twigs.

HANGING
PLANT SHELVES

Plants have a delightful way of adding charm and hospitality to a room, no matter what the decorating scheme may be. Placed on a hanging plant shelf, the plants receive the necessary light and serve as an attractive window treatment. Located near the top of the window, a single hanging shelf with several hanging or climbing plants becomes a valance. A double or triple hanging shelf, hung to cover the entire window or just the lower half, acts as a curtain when filled with plants.

The shelves, made from 1 × 6 stock lumber, are braced with parting stop at each end and suspended with rope from a wooden pole. When the pole is mounted at the top of a wide window, an additional brace and rope can be added to the center, along with a center support bracket for the pole.

The ropes are knotted just below the pole and under each brace to keep the shelf hanging level. If desired, holes can be cut into the shelf to hold pots that have slanted sides and collars, such as standard clay pots. Vary the number of the shelves and the space between them, depending on the size of the window, the height of the plants, and the desired placement of the plant shelves.

Holes cut into this hanging plant shelf hold potted plants of various colors, sizes, and shapes.

SELECTING PLANTS

Select plants for the hanging shelf according to the light requirements of the plants. Also consider other habits and features of the plants, such as the plant colors, their direction of growth, the size they will become, and their tolerance. Place plants of different sizes, shapes, and colors next to each other for contrast, or place several similar plants together for a more uniform look.

MATERIALS

- 1 × 6 boards, preferably of grade #2 or better.
- Parting stop.
- 180-grit or 220-grit sandpaper.
- Drill and 5/16" drill bit; 3/32" combination drill and countersink bit.
- 6 × 1" (2.5 cm) flat-head sheet-metal screws.
- 3/16" (4.5 mm) nylon or polyester rope.

- Wood pole, 1⅜" (3.5 cm) in diameter, and finials.
- Pole brackets with 4" to 6" (10 to 15 cm) projection; center support bracket for pole measuring 36" (91.5 cm) or more, mounted at the top of a window.
- Latex paint, or wood stain and clear acrylic finish; sponge applicator.

CUTTING DIRECTIONS

Cut a 1 × 6 board for each shelf, with the length of the board equal to the outside measurement of the window frame. For the end braces under each shelf, cut two 7" (18 cm) lengths of parting stop. If the shelves are more than 36" (91.5 cm) wide, cut a third brace for the center of each shelf.

Mount the brackets for the wood pole as on page 41, step 10. Then, cut the wood pole 2" (5 cm) longer than the distance from the outer edge of one bracket to the outer edge of the other bracket. Cut a piece of rope for each end and for the center, if needed, with the length equal to twice the distance from the top of the pole to the bottom of the lowest shelf plus 6" (15 cm) for the upper knot plus 6" (15 cm) for each knot under each shelf plus an extra 6" to 10" (15 to 25.5 cm). Wrap tape around the cords before cutting, to prevent raveling.

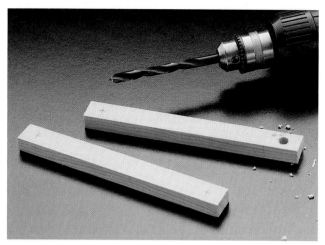

1 Mark placement of holes for rope on the wide side of braces, ½" (1.3 cm) from each end; drill holes, using 5/16" drill bit.

2 Sand all wood surfaces, using 180-grit or 220-grit sandpaper; round the corners of the shelves and braces slightly.

3 Mark lines on underside of shelf 2" (5 cm) from each end. On wide side of braces, mark placement for screws, 1½" (3.8 cm) from ends. Place braces, wide side up, on shelf, with outer edges along lines and ends extending equally on each side of shelf. Position a third brace, if needed, at center of board. Repeat for braces on any additional shelves.

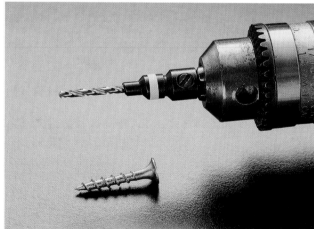

4 Adjust 3/32" combination drill and countersink bit as shown, so head of the drywall screw will be recessed below surface of wood when inserted into drilled hole; tighten set screw.

5 Predrill screw holes, holding the brace firmly in place as positioned in step 3; drill through brace and into underside of shelf, up to point on drill bit indicated by white line. Insert 6 × 1" (2.5 cm) drywall screw. Repeat for remaining braces.

6 Paint the shelves, if desired, or stain shelves and apply clear acrylic finish.

7 Fold the ropes in half. Tie each folded rope together in an overhand knot near the folded end, leaving a 2½" (6.5 cm) loop; tie all knots in the same direction so they look the same. Place ropes on work surface, aligning the ends and knots.

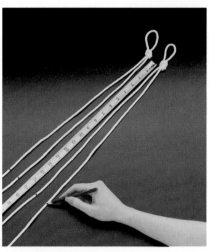

8 Measure from the overhand knots to the desired location for the first set of shelf support knots, allowing 1¼" (3.2 cm) for the thickness of the shelf and braces. Mark the ropes with pencil.

9 Thread the rope down through the holes in the braces of the shelf until the pencil marks are below the braces. As shown, tie a figure-eight knot at each location, just under mark.

10 Repeat steps 8 and 9 for any additional shelves, measuring from previous knots. Mount brackets for wood pole, either on the window frame or just outside the frame; use molly bolts or toggle anchors if not installing the brackets into window frame or wall studs. If a center support bracket is needed, mount it with one side of bracket at center.

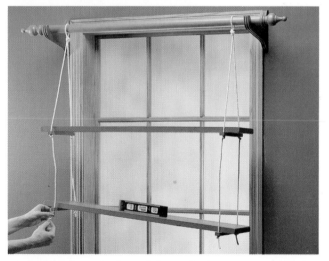

11 Slide the pole through loops in the rope, and attach finials to ends; mount the pole on brackets. Check to see that shelves are level and resting on knots; adjust the knots if necessary. Trim excess rope under the knots for the bottom shelf.

HOW TO MAKE A HANGING PLANT SHELF WITH INSERTED POTS

1 Mark placement for the ropes and drill holes as on page 40, step 1. Measure the circumference of flowerpot just under collar. Divide this measurement by 6.28 to determine radius. Draw a circle with this radius on paper, using a compass.

2 Cut out the circle; slide it over the bottom of the pot up to the collar; adjust the size of the hole, if necessary.

3 Determine the number of holes and spacing between them; the outer edge of first and last holes should be at least 3½" (9 cm) from the end of the shelf, and the minimum spacing between holes is 2" (5 cm). Mark circles for the holes on top of the shelf.

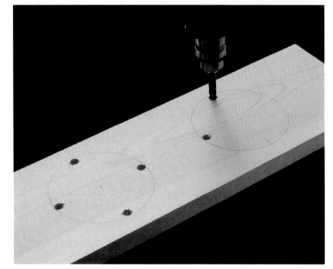

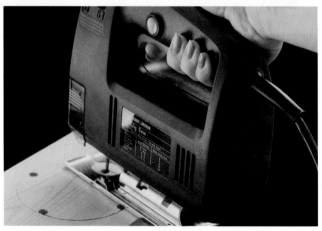

4 Drill four evenly spaced holes at inner edge of each circle, using large drill bit.

5 Insert jigsaw blade into drilled hole; cut on marked line up to next hole. Turn board, and continue sawing, turning board at each hole until entire circle is cut out. Repeat for remaining holes. Complete plant shelf as on pages 40 and 41, steps 2 to 11.

MORE IDEAS FOR PLANT WINDOW TREATMENTS

Potted ivy plants, *hung at the sides of a window, climb the honeysuckle vine over the window frame. Secure the honeysuckle vines by wrapping them with wire and twisting the wire around screw eyes inserted into the window frame or wall. Loosely tie ivy stems to the honeysuckle vine, using string or plant ties; train new growth to climb by gently weaving it through the vine.*

Spider plants *(above), suspended from the ceiling at different heights, create an arched valance. The plant hangers with clear monofilament line are hung from ceiling hooks.*

African violets *(right) are hung at the sides of tieback curtains, using wall brackets designed for holding pots.*

HANGING BASKETS

For a lush hanging basket overflowing with flowers, make an arrangement using a wire-frame basket. The flowers are planted not only at the top of the basket, but also at the sides for a fuller effect. The open framework of the wire basket allows the plants to be inserted at various levels, and, once mature, the plants will conceal the frame.

Wire baskets are available at garden centers in a variety of sizes, generally ranging from 8" to 20" (20.5 to 51 cm) in diameter. Although the baskets themselves are lightweight, once filled and well watered, hanging baskets can become quite heavy. Make sure the basket is suspended from a bracket or hook that is securely anchored. To reduce the weight, use a soilless planting mix.

Because hanging baskets need frequent watering, hang them in a convenient location. Add a plastic lining between the moss and the potting mix to help retain the moisture.

When selecting the plants for the hanging basket, choose a combination of bushy and trailing plants that complement each other. To maintain the arrangement, regularly trim off any dead flowers and leaves as well as any overvigorous plant growth.

MATERIALS

- Several plants in combination of bushy and trailing varieties.
- Wire basket.
- Sheet moss.
- Black plastic sheeting.
- Plastic wrap.
- Soilless potting mix.
- Wire plant hanger, or metal chains and S-hooks.
- Wall bracket or ceiling hook.

HOW TO MAKE A HANGING BASKET

1 Line wire basket with sheet moss, placing large piece in bottom of basket and tearing off smaller pieces to fit along sides; overlap pieces, and extend moss to the upper edge of basket.

2 Place plastic sheet inside the basket, over the moss; trim plastic about ¾" (2 cm) below upper edge of the basket. Cut small slashes in plastic near the base, for drainage. Where plants will be inserted, cut X-shaped slashes through plastic and moss, at various levels in lower half of basket. Fill basket with potting mix, up to the X-shaped slashes.

3 Secure wire plant hanger to basket, spacing wires evenly; wrap and twist ends securely. Or secure three lengths of metal chain to basket; secure ends of chain to S-hook.

4 Wrap a plant loosely with a sheet of plastic wrap; this allows you to easily insert the plant through the slash in the plastic and moss.

5 Insert foliage of the plant, from inside of basket, through the slash in plastic and moss. Remove plastic wrapping, and carefully spread the roots apart inside basket. Repeat for remaining slashes. Fill basket partway with potting mix, allowing space for the plants on the top of the basket.

6 Arrange the plants as desired on top of basket, distributing them evenly so the basket will hang level; surround plants with potting mix. Fill in any remaining space in basket with potting mix, leaving at least ½" (1.3 cm) of space at top for watering.

7 Fill in the spaces between the plants with moss; this helps hold moisture between waterings. Hang basket from wall bracket or ceiling hook. Water thoroughly.

SETTINGS FOR
CONTAINER GARDENS

Container gardens are so portable and versatile that they can be located virtually anywhere, even in unexpected areas. To create an appealing setting, give some thought to the placement of the containers. An ordinary concrete patio can become a picturesque environment with container gardening. Or a basic privacy fence can come alive with foliage in hanging baskets.

When planning a container garden, group several containers together for greater impact. To create a multilevel garden, take advantage of existing stairs or use pedestals and benches to display plantings. For depth, stagger the placement of the containers rather than align them in a straight row.

CREATIVE CONTAINERS

To personalize container gardens, use nontraditional containers rather than the standard planters and pots found in garden centers. For old-fashioned, rustic appeal, consider using quaint found items, such as tin watering cans, old wheelbarrows, and wooden crates. Or create a fanciful, picturesque patio garden, using a collection of pretty teapots. The choice of containers is unlimited.

Depending on the found items you choose, you may want to plant directly into the containers or simply insert prepotted plants. Some items, including old colanders and wire baskets, provide the proper drainage for plants, while others may require a layer of pebbles at the bottom of the container to protect the plant's root system from water damage.

Pair of teapots (above), used as flowerpots, are arranged on a patio table.

Grapevine wreaths, stacked around a plastic ice cream bucket, create a container with a woodsy look. Tuck moss into the wreaths for added texture.

Colander *hung from a tree branch contains petunias and variegated vinca plants.*

Picnic basket, *filled with favorite annuals, becomes a unique container. Plant flowers in flowerpots, and insert a dish in the bottom of the basket to collect any water seepage from drainage holes.*

Fishing creel (above) stuffed with flowerpots hangs on a porch wall.

Cowboy boots (right) are used as holders for a cactus and other potted plants.

Old wagon and sprinkling can (below) are filled with plants and grouped together for a clever garden setting.

Silks & Other
Artificials

SILK FLOWERS

Silk is the general term used to describe any artificial floral materials, including those made of silk, polyester, parchment, or latex. Silk flowers usually have wired stems, making them flexible; the wire stems are covered with floral tape or plastic. Flowers with plastic stems are more economical. Silk flowers are available at most floral shops, garden centers, and craft stores.

Ranunculus

Anthurium

Daisy

Wild rose

Iris

Statice

Miniature roses

Larkspur

Delphinium

Forsythia

Hydrangeas

Baby's breath

Peony

Gingerroot heliconia

Freesia

Sunflower

Alstroemeria

Begonia

Bird of paradise

Rose

Sweet william

Lilac

Astilbe

SILK FOLIAGE, BERRIES & FRUIT

Leafy silk, or artificial, foliage is available in a variety of shapes and colors. Artificial berries and fruit, often of latex, papier-mâché, or plastic, are available in clusters, attached to vines, and as individual items.

Marsh berries

Ginkgo

Ivy

Autumn foliage

Begonia

Pumpkin vine

Caladium

Bear grass

Rose hip

Grapes

Pear

SINGLE-VARIETY ARRANGEMENTS

A single variety of flowers, displayed in a vase, makes a simple arrangement with dramatic impact. Several blossoms in one color can be stunning. To achieve the look of fresh-cut flowers, display the arrangement in a clear glass container.

HOW TO MAKE A
SINGLE-VARIETY ARRANGEMENT

MATERIALS

- Silk irises or other flowers.
- Clear glass container.
- Clear marbles.

- Floral Styrofoam® for silk arranging.
- Floral adhesive clay.
- Wire cutter; serrated knife.

1 Insert floral Styrofoam for silk arranging into glass container; cover with marbles (page 23).

2 Insert flowers into foam, spacing evenly around container and varying heights. Bend stems slightly downward near outer edges for natural appearance.

Single stems, each in its own vase, are grouped together for impact.

MORE IDEAS FOR SINGLE-VARIETY ARRANGEMENTS

Several colors *of a single variety make a bold statement when placed in a colorful, artistic vase.*

Artificial bulbs *are placed in specially designed glass vases. Crocus flowers are inserted into the bulbs for a realistic look.*

SILK CENTERPIECES

Centerpieces are designed to be seen from all sides and are therefore usually symmetrical in shape. Made from silk materials, centerpieces may be seasonal displays of color or they may be used year-round. They can vary in height or size, depending on their intended use. Low arrangements are ideal on a dining room table, while taller arrangements create a dramatic display on a sofa table or pedestal.

HOW TO MAKE A SILK CENTERPIECE

MATERIALS

- Silk roses or other dominant flowers.
- Silk rosebuds or other secondary flowers.
- Silk sweet william or other filler flowers.
- Marsh berries or other filler material.
- Silk begonia or other flowering leafy plant.

- Brass pot or other container.
- Floral Styrofoam® for silk arranging.
- Spanish moss.
- Wire cutter; serrated knife.
- Floral pins.

1 Insert foam into container, and cover (page 23). Insert roses into foam, spacing them evenly. Bend stems and leaves as necessary to give flowers a natural appearance.

2 Cut begonia plant apart at base of stems, using wire cutter. Extend length of stems with wire or picks as necessary (page 24); insert into arrangement, spacing evenly.

3 Insert rosebuds evenly throughout arrangement so the centerpiece appears balanced from all angles.

4 Cut sweet william stems to desired lengths; insert flowers evenly into arrangement to fill in any bare areas.

5 Insert the stems of marsh berries evenly. Adjust flowers or leaves to balance the design and give a natural appearance.

Three-sided arrangements are designed to be used against a wall or in a corner of a room. Use silk flowers and foliage to create the triangular design shown here, following the instructions below. Or make any of the other basic arrangements on pages 6 and 7 by inserting the materials as necessary to achieve the desired form.

HOW TO MAKE A THREE-SIDED SILK ARRANGEMENT

MATERIALS

- Silk daisies or other dominant flowers.
- Silk ranunculus and grape hyacinth or other secondary flowers.
- Silk desert candle or other filler flowers.
- Silk variegated ivy or other foliage.

- Silk forsythia or other line material.
- Brass pot or other container.
- Floral Styrofoam® for silk arranging.
- Wire cutter; serrated knife; floral pins.

1 Insert foam into container, and cover (page 23). Insert forsythia into foam, placing one tall stem in center and one short stem on each side to establish height and width. Adjust length of stems, if desired.

2 Continue inserting forsythia, and insert ivy into the arrangement, creating desired shape; place some of the materials at the back. Materials in the center point upward, and materials on the sides point outward.

3 Insert daisies into arrangement, spacing evenly throughout to keep arrangement balanced on three sides.

4 Insert ranunculus and grape hyacinth evenly, one variety at a time, so the arrangement appears balanced.

5 Insert desert candle into arrangement to fill in any bare areas.

S-CURVE
ARRANGEMENTS

An asymmetrical S-curve arrangement can be viewed from three sides, and therefore works well placed against a wall or in a corner. The design is formed by shaping the silk line material into an S form. Dominant flowers are inserted within the curved design, then bare areas filled in with filler flowers and foliage to complete the arrangement.

HOW TO MAKE AN S-CURVE ARRANGEMENT

MATERIALS

- Silk delphinium or other line material.
- Silk roses or other dominant flowers.
- Silk statice and hydrangeas or other filler flowers.
- Tall vase or other container.

- Floral Styrofoam® for silk arranging.
- Spanish moss.
- Wire cutter; serrated knife.
- Floral pins.

1 Insert foam in container, and cover with moss (page 23). Insert the silk delphinium, placing some on the left side, pointing upward, and some on right side, draping downward. Shape stems into an S shape.

2 Cut one rose stem short, placing it in the center toward front of the container; trim off any excess leaves; set aside. Insert the remaining roses, bending the stems as necessary to maintain the desired S shape.

3 Insert the stems of hydrangeas to fill in the S shape. Longer stems curve upward on left side and downward on right; stems of flowers in the center are cut short to maintain the shape of the design.

4 Insert the statice, spacing evenly along curve. Tuck any remaining leaves into the center of the arrangement to fill any bare areas. Bend the stems as necessary to maintain the S shape.

MORE IDEAS FOR SILK ARRANGEMENTS

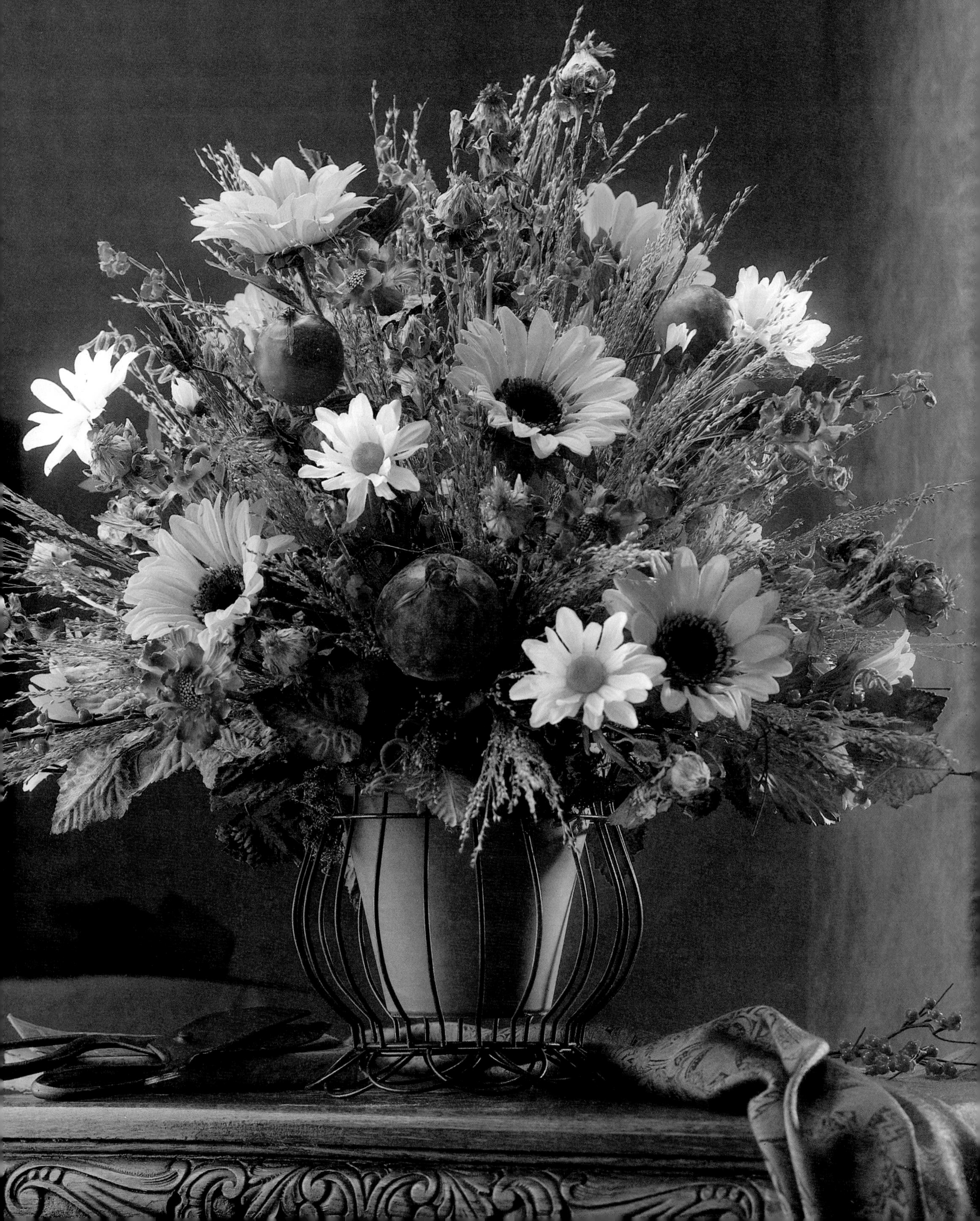

Autumn colors *dominate the floral arrangement opposite, which combines both silk and dried floral materials for textural interest. The rustic look is emphasized by the terra-cotta and wire container.*

Opposite colors *on the color wheel are used to create a dramatic display in the elegant vase at right. Silk ranunculus, snapdragons, and irises are combined with dried Queen Anne's lace.*

Spring colors *are used in the crescent arrangement below. Line materials are shaped to give the design its form.*

TROPICAL ARRANGEMENTS

Tropical flowers make a dramatic statement. Although usually arranged asymmetrically as shown here, tropical arrangements are occasionally symmetrical (page 71). Tropical arrangements often complement contemporary interiors; however, small arrangements can be suitable for other decorating styles, and a party may be an excellent opportunity to use tropical silk flowers as a decorating accent.

HOW TO MAKE AN ASYMMETRICAL TROPICAL ARRANGEMENT

MATERIALS

- Silk gingerroot heliconia, birds of paradise, and anthurium or other dominant flowers.
- Silk ti leaves, variegated plants, and caladium plants or other foliage.
- Dried lotus pods or other pods.

- Low container.
- Floral Styrofoam® for silk arranging.
- Spanish moss.
- Wire cutter; serrated knife; floral pins.

1 Insert foam into container, and cover (page 23). Insert two ti leaves on right side and two on the left; insert one into center, pointing upward. Shape leaves as desired.

2 Insert some variegated leaves into center to give height, and insert additional stems in the front and on the right. Insert caladium leaves around the rim to fill in any bare areas.

3 Group flowers by variety to make each more noticeable, placing the gingerroot heliconia in center at varying heights and anthurium on the right side.

4 Cut two bird of paradise stems short; insert on left side at the front of container. Place one in the center, keeping height about the same as gingerroot heliconia. Insert lotus pods cut to varying heights on the right side of arrangement to add texture and visual weight.

MORE IDEAS FOR TROPICAL ARRANGEMENTS

Tropical varieties in burgundy and white are mixed with bear grass and plumosa, to make an elegant arrangement. They are placed in a gold mesh vase that has been decorated with a matching cord and tassels.

Large tropicals (right) in orange and red are used together for bold impact. Combine birds of paradise, protea, and gingerroot heliconia to create this dramatic display.

Orchids (left) are arranged vertically in a glass vase. The design is softened by adding curly willow and bear grass. Because of the symmetrical shape and the cut-glass vase, this arrangement works well in a traditional room.

Mixed tropicals including anthurium, devil's claw heliconia, birds of paradise, and orchids are combined for a dramatic asymmetrical design. Curly willow is added for visual interest.

PLANTSCAPES

Plants and trees provide visual contrast and are often used to soften the lines of a room. Placed in groupings called *plantscapes,* they can make beautiful displays. A single plant, such as an ivy, is effective when draped over a hutch or nestled on a shelf among a grouping of collectibles. Larger plants and trees are used in the corners of a room or fill spaces between furnishings.

Silk plants may be used in areas where it would be difficult to grow live plants, such as beneath a sofa table or on top of an armoire. Silk plants require little maintenance or care. Arrangements or groupings of silk plants can easily be changed from season to season, simply by replacing one plant or flower in a grouping with another.

Ferns (above), are potted identically and used for balance on a mantel.

Seasonal flowers are combined with a variety of leafy silk plants. The plantscape can easily be adapted for other seasons by replacing peonies and geraniums with poinsettias, sunflowers, or daffodils.

Ivy is draped over a hutch to soften the hard edges of the furniture.

Ficus tree (left) is the focus of a floor plantscape. Honeysuckle vines spiral around the tree and are secured with floral wire. Silk plants are arranged at the base of the ficus. An additional potted plant sits near the ficus to complete the plantscape.

Silk houseplants, grouped on a table, help to unify a collection of ceramics.

Dried
Naturals

DRIED FLOWERS & GRAINS

Dried floral materials, sometimes called dried naturals, are natural materials that have been dehydrated so they will last for long periods of time. When fresh flowers are air dried, they often shrink in size, their colors soften, and they have a more textured appearance. Flowers that are dried in silica gel or that are preserved by freeze drying often retain their original shape, although their colors may change slightly. Dried floral materials are available at many floral shops, garden centers, and craft stores. Or you may dry your own, as on pages 82 to 85.

Pepper grass

Lavender

Wheat

Mixed herbs

Limonium

Rushes

Leptosporum

Strawflowers

Hydrangea

Zinnias

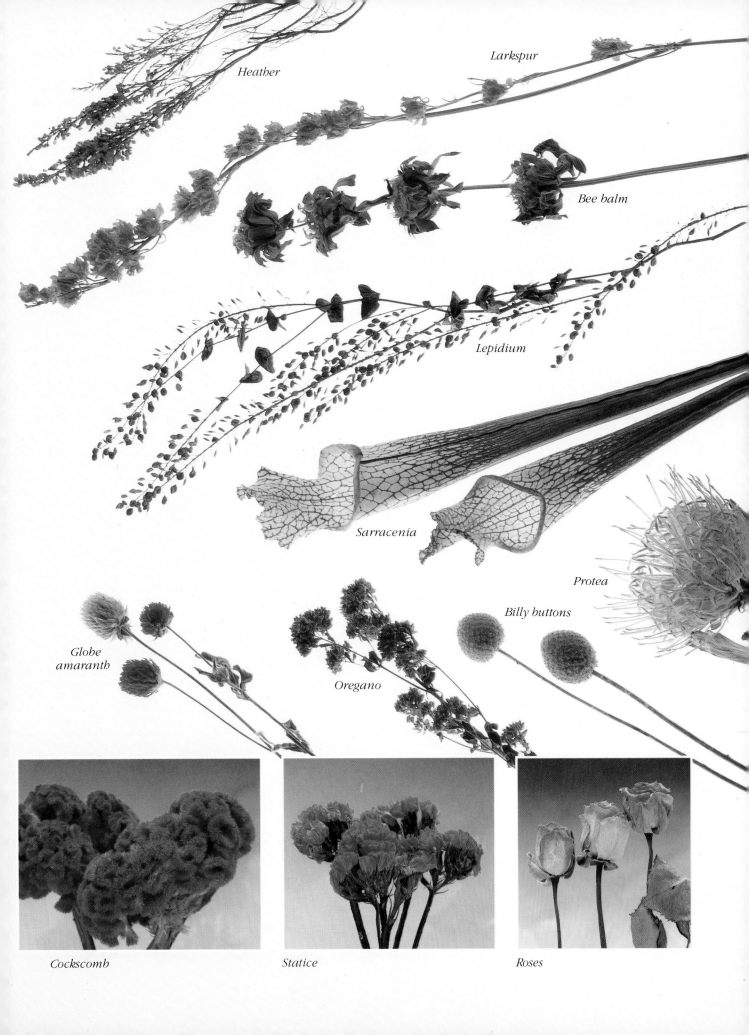

Heather

Larkspur

Bee balm

Lepidium

Sarracenia

Protea

Billy buttons

Globe
amaranth

Oregano

Cockscomb

Statice

Roses

DRIED FOLIAGE

Dried foliage is available in many varieties. Some fresh foliage can be air dried, as on page 84. Other varieties can be preserved in glycerine, which makes them more flexible and less brittle to work with. Dried and preserved foliage is available at many floral shops, garden centers, and craft stores.

Boston fern

Huckleberry with brake fern

Seeded eucalyptus

Galax

Leatherleaf

Spiral eucalyptus

Maidenhair fern

Silver-dollar eucalyptus

Protea

Boxwood

Bear grass

Salal

DRIED BERRIES, PODS & MORE

Many varieties of dried berries, pods, cones, and fruit are available at floral shops, garden centers, and craft stores. You can dry your own materials, as on page 84.

Artichoke

Honeysuckle vines

Assorted nuts

Lotus pods

Garlic bulb

Pepper berries

Poppy pods

Assorted cones

Nigella pods

Canella berries

Pomegranates

DRYING FLOWERS

Limonium *Flax* *Delphinium* *Caspia*

Air drying *on mesh works well for billy buttons, protea, and sunflowers.*

Drying your own floral materials gives you a wider range of materials to work with when making floral arrangements. Floral materials can be air dried or dried in silica gel. Air-dried flowers may be dried with their stems attached; when dry, the flowers will be smaller than their original size, and the petals and leaves will have a wrinkled appearance. Flowers dried in silica gel are dried without their stems; after drying, wire stems may be added (page 24). Flowers dried in silica gel retain the appearance of fresh flowers and remain close to their original shapes and sizes.

AIR DRYING

There are several air-drying methods for floral materials. Most varieties can be dried by hanging them upside down (above). Leaves, branches, mosses, and seed pods are usually dried flat. Some materials, such as ornamental grasses, dry well when they are set upright in a container, allowing them to bend naturally.

Other materials are dried upright in a container with a small amount of water; the water slows the drying time and helps materials retain their shapes and colors. Floral materials with large heads, such as artichokes, protea, and sunflowers, are dried by supporting the heads on wire mesh. Materials that break easily after they are dried, such as heather, boxwood, and salal, can be arranged while they are still fresh and left to dry in the arrangement.

The drying time of floral materials varies, depending on the density of and moisture in the materials, as well as the temperature and humidity of the environment. The drying time can range from a few days to several weeks; most materials dry within five days to two weeks.

When drying floral materials, place them in a location that is dark, dry, and well ventilated. Once dried, they can be stored as on pages 20 and 21.

Liatris *Mimosa* *Heather* *Bachelor's buttons*

SILICA-GEL DRYING

Available at many floral shops and craft stores, silica gel is a powder that dries flower heads to a nearly fresh appearance within a few days. It absorbs moisture from the flowers while supporting them in their natural shapes. The silica gel can be reused several times.

For best results, select flowers just before they reach full bloom; most flowers dried in full bloom do not retain their colors as well and have a tendency to fall apart when dry. If using flowers from a garden, pick them when they contain the least amount of moisture, usually early in the morning or late in the afternoon. Flowers that are deep pink, orange, yellow, blue, or purple retain their colors well. Red flowers tend to turn

Silica-gel drying *works well for peonies, roses, and asters.*

black when dry, and pastels and whites may turn brown.

The necessary drying time varies. Flowers with thin petals may dry in two to three days; dense flower heads may take five to seven days. Check the flowers every day while they are drying, so they do not overdry and become brittle.

Flowers dried in silica gel are very fragile. Handle them carefully when making the arrangement, inserting them last whenever possible. Store any extra flowers in a box, as on pages 20 and 21. Place a small amount of silica gel in the bottom of the box to absorb any moisture and keep the flowers dry.

HOW TO AIR DRY FLOWERS

Drying upright without water.
Place branches or grasses in a dry container; allow to dry.

Drying upright with water. Pour water into vase to depth of 2" (5 cm). Remove the lower leaves of floral materials, and place materials upright in vase; allow to dry. Water evaporates, leaving flowers preserved.

Drying upright on wire mesh.
Place wire mesh over deep box. Insert flower stems through mesh, allowing flower heads to rest on mesh. Support flower heads with tissue paper, if necessary.

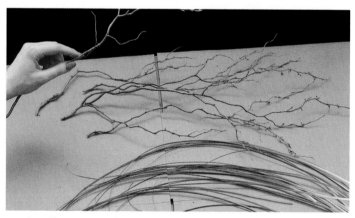

Drying flat. Lay grasses, twigs, leaves, or mosses flat on cardboard or newspaper; allow to dry. Turn the materials over occasionally, to ensure even drying.

METHODS FOR AIR DRYING FLOWERS

SUGGESTED METHOD	VARIETIES
DRYING UPRIGHT WITHOUT WATER	Branches; cattails; ornamental grasses; pussy willow; sea lavender.
DRYING UPRIGHT WITH WATER	Baby's breath; bear grass; hybrid delphiniums; hydrangea; mimosa; Queen Anne's lace.
DRYING UPRIGHT ON WIRE MESH	Billy buttons; globe artichokes; peonies; protea; roses; sunflowers.
DRYING UPSIDE DOWN	Bells of Ireland; caspia; globe amaranth; grains; herbs; larkspur; lavender; liatris; mimosa; nigella; peonies; roses; statice.
DRYING FLAT	Bear grass; branches; leaves; mosses; seed pods.

Drying upside down. Select flowers just before they reach full bloom. Remove lower leaves; trim damaged areas. Bundle flowers together loosely, staggering flower heads so air can circulate evenly. Secure bundle near ends of stems with rubber band; hang to dry.

HOW TO DRY FLOWERS IN SILICA GEL

MATERIALS

- Flower heads.
- Silica gel; airtight container.
- Newspaper; wire cutter.
- Slotted spoon; soft-bristle paintbrush.

1 Cut stems to within 1" (2.5 cm) of flower heads. Fill container with silica gel, to a depth of 1½" to 2" (3.8 to 5 cm).

2 Place flowers face up in silica gel. Gently sprinkle silica gel between flower petals.

3 Cover flowers completely with silica gel. Cover tightly with lid; allow to dry for two to seven days. Check daily, while drying, so flowers do not overdry and become brittle.

4 Remove flowers from silica gel by tipping container and gently pouring some of the silica gel onto a newspaper. When flowers are visible, gently lift them from silica gel with a slotted spoon.

5 Remove any excess silica gel from the flower petals with a soft brush. Attach any fallen petals with glue. Spray the flowers with aerosol floral sealer (page 19). Dry the silica gel, following manufacturer's directions, so it may be reused.

DRIED CENTERPIECES

Create beautiful centerpieces that fit into a variety of settings, depending on the materials you select. Use delicate dried florals and preserved airy greens for an arrangement with a touch of romance; or use dried pods, cattails, and grains to bring the country indoors.

Centerpieces are usually symmetrical in shape, since they are designed to be seen from all sides. To keep the design balanced, step away from the arrangement occasionally while creating it, and reposition the flowers, if necessary.

HOW TO MAKE A DRIED CENTERPIECE

MATERIALS

- Dried cockscomb and roses or other dominant flowers.
- Dried hydrangeas or other secondary flowers.
- Dried poppy pods and two colors of larkspur or other filler materials.
- Dried lepidium or other line material.
- Preserved maidenhair fern and galax leaves or other foliage.
- Container.
- Floral foam for dried arranging.
- Spanish moss.
- Wire cutter; serrated knife; floral pins.

1 Insert floral foam into container, and cover (page 23). Insert the lepidium into foam, establishing the shape of the arrangement.

2 Insert galax leaves into center to fill in any bare areas. Insert the cockscomb into the arrangement, spacing it evenly throughout.

3 Insert roses, spacing them evenly throughout; add wire to stems, if necessary (page 24). Insert hydrangeas, spacing them evenly throughout, filling in the rounded shape.

4 Insert poppy pods for contrast, spacing them evenly throughout. Insert larkspur, one color at a time, spacing evenly.

5 Insert maidenhair fern to fill in any bare areas; allow it to drape downward slightly.

THREE-SIDED DRIED ARRANGEMENTS

A three-sided arrangement is meant to be placed against a wall or other surface, so only three sides are visible. To preserve the look of fresh flowers, the protea are dried in silica gel as on page 85. Potpourri decoratively fills the space between the clear glass container and the floral foam.

HOW TO MAKE A THREE-SIDED DRIED ARRANGEMENT

MATERIALS

- Dried protea or other dominant flowers.
- Dried billy buttons or other secondary flowers.
- Dried salal, protea leaves, and fern or other dried foliage.
- Curly willow.
- Glass container.
- Floral foam for dried arranging.
- Potpourri; Spanish moss.
- Wire cutter; serrated knife; floral adhesive clay; anchor pin.

1 Insert floral foam into container (page 23); allow space around all sides. Fill area between the foam and the container with potpourri. Sprinkle some potpourri over top of foam.

2 Add wire stems to protea (page 25). Insert protea, then billy buttons, into foam, spacing evenly. Insert taller flowers toward the back and shorter flowers around sides and front.

3 Insert dried foliage, one variety at a time, to fill in any bare areas; keep taller stems toward back. Insert curly willow at back of arrangement to emphasize height. Tuck Spanish moss around rim of container.

MORE IDEAS FOR DRIED ARRANGEMENTS

Watering can *contains a three-sided country arrangement of wheat, eucalyptus, roses, and grapes.*

Garden basket *is created with mixed hydrangeas and stems of larkspur. Bells of Ireland add textural interest to the centerpiece.*

Crystal bowl complements a festive centerpiece of preserved boxwood, cedar, and silver-dollar eucalyptus. Pink roses and pepper berries add color to the arrangement, while pinecones and lotus pods give textural interest. The pinecones are attached to wire stems that have been covered with floral tape.

Brass pot (below) holds dried materials and artificial fruit Line materials establish the shape of the three-sided design.

Painted metal container contrasts with the bright flowers of the centerpiece. Heather and cockscomb are combined with clusters of roses and globe amaranth.

WILLOW
ARRANGEMENTS

Arrangements of dried branches are a popular room accent. Curly willow branches are especially attractive because of their gnarled, twisted look. Available from floral shops, the freshly harvested branches of curly willow are green, but will dry to shades of brown.

Willow branches can be displayed in various containers, from large ceramic pots to shallow willow baskets. Choose a container that complements the decorating scheme of the room. To secure the branches firmly, the willow arrangement is set in plaster of Paris.

HOW TO MAKE A WILLOW ARRANGEMENT

MATERIALS

- Curly willow branches.
- Sheet moss or Spanish moss.
- Decorative container.
- Plaster of Paris; disposable container for mixing.
- Cardboard; string or rubber bands.
- Heavy-duty aluminum foil.

1 Line container loosely with two layers of aluminum foil. If foil shows through sides of container, place moss between foil and container.

2 Cut cardboard to fit bottom of container; insert over foil. Cardboard will prevent branches from puncturing the foil. Trim branches to the desired height, cutting them at the base. Secure lower portion of branches together, using string or rubber bands.

3 Mix the plaster of Paris, following the manufacturer's instructions. Pour plaster into pot; plaster should be at least 4" (10 cm) deep. When the plaster starts to thicken, insert branches. Support branches until plaster has set.

4 Fold excess foil over plaster. Conceal plaster with moss. If using deep container, fill with crumpled newspaper; then add moss. Remove string or rubber bands after 24 hours.

Wreaths, Swags
& More

FRESH FLORAL TABLE WREATHS

Floral centerpieces add color and life to any table setting. This table wreath is easily assembled by simply covering a foam wreath form with greenery, then inserting floral stems into the foam. Displayed with pillar candles in the center, the wreath makes an impressive arrangement for a dining-room table or buffet. Floral varieties other than those shown here may be used to suit your preferences.

MATERIALS

- Ivy.
- Honeysuckle vines.
- Roses.
- Freesia.
- Statice.
- Smilax garland.
- Leatherleaf fern.
- Sheet moss.
- Foam wreath form for fresh flowers; floral pins.
- Grouping of pillar candles to fit within the center of wreath form.

HOW TO MAKE
A FRESH FLORAL TABLE WREATH

1 Soak foam wreath form in water until saturated; dampen the sheet moss. Cover wreath form with sheet moss; secure with floral pins.

2 Drape ivy stems over the wreath; secure with floral pins. Insert stems of leatherleaf fern into wreath; cut small openings in moss with a knife, if necessary, so stems can be inserted easily.

3 Cut honeysuckle vine into desired lengths. Insert both ends into the foam, maintaining curve of the vine and spacing vines randomly.

4 Cut stems of roses about 2" (5 cm) long, cutting them diagonally under water with sharp knife. Insert the stems into floral foam, spacing them evenly.

5 Cut stems of freesia about 2" (5 cm) long, cutting them diagonally with a sharp knife. Insert into floral foam, spacing them evenly. Repeat for statice, filling any bare areas.

6 Mist the wreath with water; place on layers of newspaper for several hours, to soak up excess water; or display the wreath on a platter. Place grouping of pillar candles in center of wreath.

SALAL & BOXWOOD WREATHS

Wreaths beautifully accent doors and walls, whether decorated for a particular season or embellished to coordinate with the decorating scheme of a room. Long-lasting beauty can be achieved by using everlasting foliage for the base and dried or preserved flowers for embellishments. Fresh salal or boxwood is an ideal choice for the base. About a week after the wreath is made, the leaves dry and curl, resulting in a beautiful display of medium to pale green foliage. To preserve the wreath's beauty, hang it away from humidity and direct sunlight. The foliage can be secured to either a wire or straw base, in small bunches or one stem at a time, depending on the fullness of the stems.

HOW TO MAKE A WIRE-BASE SALAL WREATH

MATERIALS

- Fresh salal.
- Dried roses or other dominant flowers.
- Preserved statice or other filler flowers.
- Wire wreath base.

- 22-gauge or 24-gauge paddle floral wire, cut in lengths of 15" to 18" (38 to 46 cm).
- Wire cutter.
- Hot glue gun and glue sticks.

1 Cut fresh salal into lengths ranging from 6" to 8" (15 to 20.5 cm). Cluster four to six lengths together, and wrap with wire. Place cluster on the wire base; secure by wrapping wire from cluster around the base, crossing it in back, and twisting ends together in front.

2 Secure additional salal clusters to base, overlapping each to conceal wire, until entire base is covered.

3 Secure embellishments to wreath, using hot glue. Insert dominant flowers first, followed by filler flowers; space all embellishments evenly throughout wreath.

4 Hang wreath in desired location, and allow to dry. Rotate wreath occasionally while drying, so the leaves curl evenly around the wreath's natural curve.

HOW TO MAKE A STRAW-BASE SALAL WREATH

MATERIALS

- Ready-made straw wreath.
- Fresh salal; fresh seeded eucalyptus.
- Dried roses and cockscomb or other dried flowers.
- Dried bear grass.
- Sheet moss.
- Wire cutter; floral pins; floral tape.
- 3" (7.5 cm) floral picks with wire.
- Hot glue gun and glue sticks.

1 Secure sheet moss to the top and sides of straw wreath, using hot glue. Mist the sheet moss lightly before securing, if desired, to make it more pliable.

2 Cut fresh salal stems to within 2" to 3" (5 to 7.5 cm) of lower leaves, using wire cutter; secure several stems to wreath, using floral pins. Stagger salal, covering inside, top, and outside of wreath.

3 Continue covering wreath with salal, overlapping as necessary to conceal floral pins. It is not necessary to cover moss entirely, since it contributes to the design.

4 Cut dried flower stems to lengths ranging from 4" to 6" (10 to 15 cm); wire them to floral picks as on page 24. Insert dried flowers into wreath as desired.

5 Insert seeded eucalyptus into wreath, securing with hot glue. Conceal ends of eucalyptus under salal, and weave branches through salal to hold them in place. Wire several stems of bear grass to floral picks, and insert into wreath as desired.

6 Hang wreath in desired location, and allow to dry. Rotate wreath occasionally while drying, so the leaves curl evenly around the wreath's natural curve.

HOW TO MAKE A WIRE-BASE OR STRAW-BASE BOXWOOD WREATH

1 Make wire-base wreath as on page 98, steps 1 and 2, or make straw-base wreath, opposite, steps 1 to 3; substitute fresh box-wood for salal. Attach embellishments such as pomegranates, roses, artichokes, pepper grass, and pepper berries to wreath, securing them with hot glue.

2 Hang wreath in desired location, and allow to dry. Rotate the wreath occasionally while drying, so leaves curl evenly around the wreath's natural curve.

CHRISTMAS WREATHS

Nothing echoes a Christmas tradition more than wreaths. You can make your own from fresh, preserved, or artificial greens. Or purchase ready-made wreaths and add your own embellishments. Fresh evergreen and eucalyptus wreaths, both easy to make, add fragrance to a room. Other wreath styles, including grapevine and twig wreaths, are available at craft and floral stores.

You may choose to embellish an entire wreath, use a third of the wreath as the design area, or add a single embellishment. It is usually more attractive if the focal point of the design is slightly offset.

Choose embellishments that are in scale with the size of the wreath, and vary the size of the embellishments so there will be a dominant focal point, with smaller items that complement it. Choose items that are harmonious in style, yet provide some contrast in color and texture. Several suggestions for embellishing wreaths are shown on pages 114 to 119.

HOW TO MAKE A FRESH EVERGREEN WREATH

MATERIALS

- Fresh greens.
- 22-gauge or 24-gauge paddle floral wire; wire cutter; pruning shears.
- Coat hanger.
- Ribbon and embellishments as desired.

1 Shape coat hanger into circle. Cut greens into sprigs. Wire three sprigs to hanger, with tips facing up, placing two in front and one in back; wrap wire at base of sprigs.

2 Continue wrapping clusters of greens with wire, overlapping each cluster to conceal wire. When coat hanger is covered, cut some full tips of greens and wire them to hanger, concealing ends of sprigs.

HOW TO MAKE A EUCALYPTUS WREATH

MATERIALS

- Ready-made straw wreath.
- Eucalyptus with fine stems; two or three bunches will be sufficient for most wreath sizes.
- 22-gauge or 24-gauge paddle floral wire; wire cutter; pruning shears.
- Ribbon and embellishments as desired.

1 Cut eucalyptus in half or in thirds, so each sprig is 6" to 7" (15 to 18 cm) long. Secure the bottom 1" (2.5 cm) of several sprigs to wreath with wire, wrapping the wire around wreath; cover front and sides of wreath.

2 Continue adding sprigs to front and sides of wreath; layer sprigs and wrap with wire, working in one direction. Stagger the length of the tips randomly.

3 Lift tips of sprigs at starting point, and secure last layer of sprigs under them. Make a wire loop for hanging; secure loop to back of the wreath. Embellish as desired.

EASY GRAPEVINE WREATHS

Make eye-catching wreaths to enhance any decorating style, using simple grapevine wreaths and artificial floral material. Embellish a wreath with silk ivy garlands for instant freshness. Attach lush stems of latex fruits and berries, complete with leaves and curly vines. For a woodsy effect, create a focal point on a grapevine wreath by clustering assorted bird's nests. To make a blooming wreath, purchase silk blooming plants, which are more economical and have more leaves than individual flower stems. Secure all embellishments to the grapevine wreath quickly and easily, using a hot glue gun or floral wire.

MATERIALS

- Grapevine wreath.
- Hot glue gun and glue sticks; floral wire.
- Silk ivy garland, large-leafed stems, raffia, for foliage wreath.

- Stems of latex fruit and berries with leaves and curly vines, 1 yd. to 2 yd. (0.95 to 1.85 m) ribbon, optional, for wreath with fruit and berries.
- Bird's nests in assorted shapes and sizes, dried baby's breath, for wreath with clustered nests.
- Silk blooming plants, wire cutter, 2½ yd. to 3 yd. (2.3 to 2.75 m) ribbon, for blooming wreath.

HOW TO MAKE A FOLIAGE WREATH

1 Wrap ivy garland around grapevine wreath; secure, using hot glue as needed.

2 Cut single leaves from large-leafed stems. Arrange leaves throughout wreath as desired; secure, using hot glue.

3 Tie several strands of raffia into bow with long tails; secure to top of wreath, using floral wire or hot glue.

HOW TO MAKE A WREATH WITH FRUIT & BERRIES

1 Arrange several stems of fruit and berries around the grapevine wreath, inserting stems into the wreath and clustering them more heavily in one area to create a focal point; secure, using hot glue.

2 Weave a ribbon around the wreath, if desired, arranging twists and loops; secure with hot glue as necessary.

HOW TO MAKE A WREATH WITH CLUSTERED NESTS

1 Arrange bird's nests in cluster near center of grapevine wreath; secure, using floral wire or hot glue.

2 Apply hot glue to sprigs of baby's breath; insert into grapevine and around nests for accent.

HOW TO MAKE A BLOOMING WREATH

1 Cut flower stems from silk blooming plant. Arrange flowers evenly around wreath, inserting stems into wreath; secure, using hot glue.

2 Cut leafy stems from plant. Fill in areas around flowers with leaves, inserting stems into wreath; secure, using hot glue.

3 Make cluster bow with long tails (below). Secure bow to wreath, using floral wire. Trail tails of bow through flowers and leaves, securing as necessary.

HOW TO MAKE A CLUSTER BOW

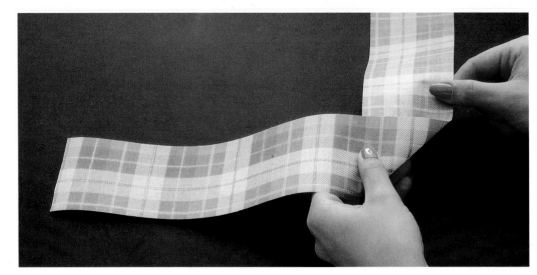

1 Place thumb and index finger at determined length for tail, with the ribbon right side up. Fold ribbon back on itself at a diagonal, with wrong sides together, so ribbon forms a right angle.

2 Wrap ribbon over thumb to form center loop; secure with fingers. Twist the ribbon one-half turn at underside of loop, so right side of the ribbon faces up.

3 Form first loop. Twist ribbon one-half turn, and form loop on opposite side.

4 Continue forming loops under the previous loops, alternating sides and twisting the ribbon so the right side always faces up; make each loop slightly larger than the loop above it.

5 When final loop has been formed, insert wire through center of bow. Bend wire around ribbon at center; twist wire tightly, gathering ribbon. Hold wire firmly at the top, and turn the bow, twisting wire snug. Separate and shape the loops.

Heart wreath is embellished with sheet moss, potted roses, lavender bunches, and pepper berries.

Miniature wreaths are paired for impact. Sheet moss, pansies, and yellow rosebuds accent the wreaths for a romantic look.

Fruit wreath (opposite), wrapped with silver-dollar eucalyptus and artificial maple leaves, is covered with artificial fruit and dried fruit slices. Pinecones and sticks give the arrangement a woodsy look.

Autumn wreath has a grapevine base with added foliage. Fruits, vegetables, hydrangeas, poppy pods, and potted sunflowers embellish the wreath. Honeysuckle vine encircles the wreath.

TWIG WREATHS

Use twigs to create a wreath with a textured, woodsy look. Change the embellishments for each season, using natural items gathered from your yard or walks in the woods. Or for longer-lasting displays, embellish a twig wreath with artificial or preserved foliage. Many embellishments can be simply tucked securely within the twigs, allowing you to use the same wreath year-round. Or make several wreaths, using a variety of twigs.

MATERIALS

- Twigs and small branches; pruning shears.
- Flat wire wreath base.
- 24-gauge paddle floral wire; wire cutter.
- Natural or artificial embellishments, such as pussy-willow stems and silk ivy for spring, artificial fruit and berries for summer, autumn leaves and dried pods for fall, and pine boughs and pinecones for winter.
- Ribbon or raffia, optional.

Spring wreath (opposite), made using birch twigs, features a watering can, seed packets, and artificial vegetables. Sheet moss is tucked between the twigs for additional color.

Autumn wreath (right) is made using branches from a winged euonymus bush. A potted cactus becomes the focal point, and dried chili peppers tucked into the wreath add color.

HOW TO MAKE A TWIG WREATH

1 Cut twigs into lengths ranging from 10" to 13" (25.5 to 33 cm) long. Bundle several twigs together; wrap with paddle floral wire. Secure paddle floral wire to the wire wreath base. Place twig bundle on base, and tightly wrap with floral wire to secure.

2 Secure additional twig bundles to base, until entire base is covered; angle bundles so the twigs radiate out in one direction and cover wire of previous bundles.

3 Add seasonal embellishments; tuck items between twigs, securing with wire, if necessary.

113

Honeysuckle vine *encircles an artificial wreath. A gilded reindeer and gold bow are elegant highlights. Artichokes, cones, hydrangea, and pomegranates add textural interest.*

MORE IDEAS FOR WREATHS

Victorian wreath *made from eucalyptus (page 103) features a pearlescent cherub on a pastel satin bow. Statice and clustered pastel embellishments are used throughout the wreath.*

Dried naturals *are the primary embellishments for this twig wreath (page 112). The bird's nest, slightly off center on the wreath, becomes the focal point.*

Evergreen bouquet *of mixed greens and pinecones is wired asymmetrically onto a ready-made grapevine wreath for a quick embellishment. The narrow French ribbon is wrapped loosely around the wreath.*

Apples and popcorn *are used as the dominant embellishment for this fresh wreath of mixed greens (page 103). To carry out the natural look, nuts and pinecones are also used.*

Artificial evergreen garland *is wrapped around a grapevine wreath. A natural look is created by adding birch bark and twig birdhouses, artificial birds, and stems of rose hips.*

Gold and red metallics *are used for a dramatic effect, and the embellishments are offset for even more impact. The ready-made straw wreath used as the base was concealed with metallic ribbon and tiny garland.*

Wire-mesh bow *and metal ornaments are used to embellish a fresh evergreen wreath. The mesh strips for the bow measure about 4" (10 cm) wide and 24" (61 cm) long. Lights were added to the wreath before it was decorated.*

Village house *becomes the focal point of an artificial wreath. Additional sprigs of greenery, cones, and berries are added for texture and fullness. For a snowy effect, aerosol artificial snow is sprayed over polyester fiberfill.*

TIPS FOR EMBELLISHING WREATHS

Attach wire to a cone by wrapping the wire around bottom layers of cone. Attach wire to a cinnamon stick by inserting it through length of stick; wrap wire around stick, and twist the ends at the middle. Trim wire, leaving 6" (15 cm) ends for attaching to wreath.

Strengthen fragile stems of dried flowers with wire. Make floral or berry clusters by grouping items together. Attach wire to items as necessary. Wrap stems and wires with floral tape.

Add texture to evergreen wreaths by inserting sprigs of other evergreen varieties. Secure sprigs to the wreath base, using wire.

Display collectibles, such as village houses and ornaments, on a wreath for visual impact. Wire items securely to the wreath base.

Gild embellishments, such as twigs, cones, artichokes, and sprigs of greenery, by applying gold aerosol acrylic paint.

Embellish wreath with ribbon by weaving it through the wreath; create twists and turns for depth. Secure the ribbon as necessary with hot glue.

Wrap honeysuckle vine loosely over a wreath, for added texture. Secure the vine with floral wire or hot glue.

Wrap artificial garland around a grapevine wreath to add color and dimension.

Add battery-operated lights to a wreath by weaving the cords into the wreath boughs.

Embellish bows with additional loops of contrasting ribbon. Fold length of ribbon in half to form loop the same size as loops on the existing bow; wrap ends tightly with wire. Secure to the center of bow, using hot glue.

Shape an artificial wreath made on a single wire into a candy cane or swag. Cut the wreath apart where the wire was joined.

Add luster to pinecones by applying glossy brown aerosol paint.

Apply aerosol clear acrylic sealer to dried arrangements; protect found object with plastic wrap, if desired.

Highlight twigs, vines, and cones with frost, glitter, or glossy aerosol paint.

Join grapevine wreaths by loosening coils of one wreath; position over the remaining wreath, and arrange vines for a loose, airy effect. Attach vines to the lower wreath, using floral wire.

Keep a balanced look when embellishing an entire wreath by dividing wreath into three or four sections; distribute items evenly within each section.

FLORAL SWAGS

A floral swag may be hung either vertically or horizontally on the wall. Even small rooms usually have a vertical wall space to embellish decoratively, or a horizontal area above a mirror, a doorway, or a tall piece of furniture.

Easily constructed, this floral swag is simply wired together. Choose silk flowers with flexible stems. Select large focal flowers with thick stems to provide a sturdy base for the swag.

HOW TO MAKE A SILK FLORAL WALL SWAG

MATERIALS

- Silk lilies or other line material with large flowers.
- Silk roses or other medium-size focal materials.
- Cluster of berries and other fruit or other secondary materials.
- Silk grapevine leaves or other greenery, for filler material.
- 22-gauge paddle floral wire; wire cutter.

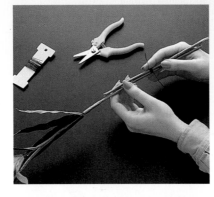

1 Place two lilies on table, aligning stems in opposite directions and overlapping them; wire the stems together, using paddle wire. Shape stems for a natural appearance.

2 Add desired number of lilies on each side, wiring one stem at a time. As each flower is added, shape stem for a natural appearance. Wire will be concealed later.

3 Wire stems of roses, one at a time, evenly spacing them throughout swag and wrapping wire tightly; shape the stems.

4 Add stems of berries and other fruit, one stem at a time, evenly spacing them throughout arrangement; wrap tightly with wire.

5 Cut short stems of silk grapevine leaves or other leaves, placing them throughout swag to conceal wires and stems of flowers and to soften the look; wire in place.

6 Shape a small wire loop; wrap wire ends around some of the stems to secure loop on the back, for hanging. For horizontal swag, position wire loop at center back; for vertical swag, position loop under the top focal flower, securing it to a heavy stem.

7 Shape the swag as necessary. Hang swag from a wire loop.

SWAGS

This vertical floral swag is both pretty and practical. Hung alone, it gracefully fills a narrow wall space. Displayed on both sides of a picture or mirror, a pair of swags can add significance to a display.

The base of the swag, made using twigs, can be constructed in many sizes. Determine the desired length and width of the twig base; then choose flowers that are appropriate for the size of the base. For proper balance, larger bases will require larger focal flowers. When making pairs of swags, insert the flowers for symmetrical arrangements.

HOW TO MAKE A SWAG

MATERIALS

- Twigs, such as birch or dogwood.
- Silk, parchment, or dried flowers in three sizes.
- Barley or other grain material.

- Grape clusters or berry stems.
- Foliage materials, such as leaves, ferns, or ivy.

- 20-gauge or 22-gauge paddle floral wire; wire cutter.
- Hot glue gun and glue sticks.

1 Cut and bundle twigs to desired finished length of swag, with tips of twigs at both ends. Wrap tightly with wire to secure. Repeat for desired finished width. Place short bundle on long bundle about one-third down from top; secure with wire. Reserve several twigs for use in step 6.

2 Insert largest flower into twig base to one side of center as shown; trim stem as necessary. Secure with hot glue.

3 Insert the remaining large flowers into the arrangement, then smaller flowers, placing flowers for a staggered vertical arrangement. Secure with hot glue.

4 Trim barley to about 7" (18 cm) in length. Cluster several stems together; secure with wire. Glue the clusters into arrangement to fill in any bare areas.

5 Insert grape clusters or berry stems, arranging them to cascade outward and downward; secure with hot glue.

6 Insert foliage materials, one variety at a time, to soften and fill out the swag. Glue additional twigs as desired for dimension and to round out shape of base. Secure wire loop for hanging to back side of swag.

A grapevine swag is easily made from a purchased grapevine wreath that has been cut in half. Hang a swag above a fireplace, or use it to decorate a wall.

Embellish the swag as desired to coordinate it with the surrounding decorating scheme. Flowers such as larkspur may replace the caspia, and a rose bundle may be substituted for the wheat sheaf.

MATERIALS

- Purchased grapevine wreath.
- Eucalyptus in two colors or other line materials.
- Dried canella berries or other desired berries.
- Dried caspia or other filler material.
- Dried wheat sheaf or other bundled material.
- 22-gauge or 24-gauge paddle floral wire; wire cutter.
- Hot glue gun and glue sticks.

HOW TO MAKE A GRAPEVINE SWAG

1 Cut the grapevine wreath in half, using a wire cutter or pruning shears. Join the halves as shown, securing them with wire.

2 Apply hot glue liberally to ends of eucalyptus, working with one color at a time; insert pieces around center of swag, spacing evenly and varying placement depth.

3 Apply glue to stems of canella berries, and insert into swag; intersperse berries among eucalyptus, varying placement depth.

4 Attach wheat sheaf to center of arrangement, applying glue generously to the sheaf and pressing it firmly into place. Hold for 5 minutes, to allow time for glue to set.

5 Apply glue to sprigs of caspia; insert into garland to fill in any bare areas as necessary.

HUCKLEBERRY
SWAGS

Swags of huckleberry can embellish any room in your home. These swags may be either arched or divided, offering two different looks. Make your own base of twigs for the arched swag shown here. Or use a purchased base for the divided swag on page 128. Embellish arched and divided swags with silk or dried flowers, or a combination of both.

Similar looks can be achieved by substituting birch, curly willow, or blueberry branches for the huckleberry. Branches of many varieties may be purchased from floral shops, or you may gather your own. Purchased swag bases are often available in birch and other branches.

HOW TO MAKE AN ARCHED HUCKLEBERRY SWAG

MATERIALS

- Huckleberry branches or other desired branches.
- Maidenhair fern and fresh heather or other fillers.
- Silk peonies or other dominant flowers.
- Dried sarracenia and silk roses or other secondary flowers.
- Grape clusters or other artificial fruit.
- Dried bear grass.
- Wire wreath base with attached wire fasteners.
- Wire cutter; floral tape.
- Hot glue gun and glue sticks.

1 Cut the wire wreath base apart, and spread it to form an arch. Secure bunches of huckleberry to the base, wrapping the wreath fasteners around bunches.

2 Cut fern into sprigs, ranging from 8" to 10" (20.5 to 25.5 cm); insert into swag at various angles, securing with hot glue. Insert heather into the swag, securing it with hot glue.

3 Cut the flower stems to lengths ranging from 6" to 10" (15 to 25.5 cm). Insert peonies, then roses, spacing them evenly throughout swag; secure with hot glue.

4 Insert grape clusters into the swag, securing them with hot glue. Insert sarracenia, spacing it evenly; secure with hot glue.

5 Make six to eight bunches of bear grass by securing ends of several stems together with floral tape. Apply glue to ends of bunches; insert, spacing them evenly to soften arrangement.

HOW TO MAKE A DIVIDED HUCKLEBERRY SWAG

MATERIALS

- Purchased divided swag base from huckleberry or other branches.
- Silk begonia or other leafy silk plant.
- Three silk delphiniums or other linear silk flowers.
- Dried rushes and leptosporum or other dried filler flowers.
- Artificial berries or other fruit.
- Wire cutter; hot glue gun and glue sticks.

1 Insert one stem of delphinium into each side of swag; secure with hot glue. Cut remaining stem of delphinium into pieces; set aside.

2 Cut rushes and leptosporum into lengths ranging from 5" to 8" (12.5 to 20.5 cm); glue some rushes to each side of swag, following the direction of the huckleberry branches and spacing evenly.

3 Cut stems from begonia plant, using wire cutter. Add floral picks, if necessary (page 24). Apply glue to the ends; insert stems evenly into the swag.

4 Insert some of the leptosporum into each side of swag; secure with glue. Fill in any bare areas with delphinium pieces. Glue the berries close to center.

GREEN
GARLANDS

Graceful swags of garland add a dramatic touch to a room. Whether the garlands are made from fresh, preserved, or artificial greens, they can be embellished for an impressive statement.

Fresh garlands are quick and easy to make, and handmade fresh garlands have a fuller shape than purchased ones. When making your own, mix different varieties of greens for added color and texture. Fresh cuttings can often be purchased by weight from nurseries. Cedar greens work especially well for indoor use; they do not shed, and they keep their color longer than most varieties.

For the realistic look of fresh garlands, use dried or preserved greens. They last longer than fresh garlands and can be used for more than one season. For a garland that can be used year after year, use artificial greens. To add the fragrance of evergreen, embellish the garland with scented pinecones or tuck in a few sprigs of fresh greens.

HOW TO MAKE A FRESH GARLAND

MATERIALS

- Fresh greens.
- Lightweight rope or twine.
- 22-gauge paddle floral wire or chenille stems.
- Pruning shears.
- Wire cutter.

2 Continue wiring greens around rope, overlapping them to conceal the wire. At desired length, wire full tips of greens to bottom of garland, concealing ends of sprigs.

1 Tie rope to solid overhead object, such as ceiling-mounted plant hook. Cut fresh greens into sprigs. Wire three sprigs to rope, with tips facing up, placing two in front and one in back; wrap wire at the base of the sprigs.

3 Cut the wire and rope at ends of garland; knot ends, forming loops for hanging, if desired.

131

FLEXIBLE GARLANDS

Garlands are versatile accessories for any room. They can be draped over headboards, shelves, pictures, or doorways. Flexible silk garlands are easily made by twisting wired flowers to an ivy garland. Nonwired materials can be attached to the garland, if desired, by securing them with floral wire.

HOW TO MAKE A FLEXIBLE GARLAND

MATERIALS

- Silk roses or other dominant flowers.
- Silk alstroemeria and astilbe or other secondary flowers.
- Silk miniature roses or other filler flowers.
- One 9-ft. (2.75 m) silk ivy garland.
- Two silk ivy plants, one solid green and one variegated.
- 22-gauge paddle floral wire and wire cutter, if silk flowers are not wired.

1 Cut stems from ivy plants; to add fullness, wrap the stems around garland, allowing some tendrils to extend.

2 Insert roses, spacing them evenly throughout the garland; secure by wrapping the stems around garland.

3 Insert astilbe into garland between roses, wrapping the stems around garland. Insert alstroemeria, spacing evenly; wrap the stems around garland.

4 Insert miniature roses to fill in any bare areas; wrap stems around garland.

SHAPED GARLANDS

Delicate-looking floral garlands add a romantic touch to walls or tables. For impact, drape a garland over a large mirror or shape one around a doorway to soften the straight lines and square corners. A shaped garland can also serve as a centerpiece when arranged down the center of a dining room table.

Create the base of the garland by encasing an evergreen garland in Spanish moss. For longer garlands, secure two or more evergreen garlands together.

MATERIALS

- One 6-ft. (1.85 m) evergreen garland.
- Silk hydrangeas and wild roses or other dominant flowers.
- Silk freesia or other secondary flowers.
- Silk baby's breath, astilbe, and wild berry sprays or other filler materials.
- Two 9-ft. (2.75 m) ivy garlands.

- Silk ivy plant.
- Berry vine.
- Spanish moss.
- Huckleberry twigs and honeysuckle vine, optional.
- Ribbon, optional.
- Fishing line.
- Wire cutter.
- Hot glue gun and glue sticks.

HOW TO MAKE A SHAPED GARLAND

1 Surround evergreen garland with Spanish moss, so the evergreen is barely visible; moss adheres to garland. Tie fishing line to garland at one end, and spiral it around the garland, encasing the moss; tie fishing line at opposite end. (White cord was used for clarity.)

2 Wrap ivy garlands around base in opposite directions, twisting vines around base to secure. Wrap berry vine around evergreen garland, allowing some tendrils to extend. Cut stems from ivy plant, and glue stems to garland, allowing some tendrils to extend.

3 Cut all flower stems to lengths ranging from 3" to 5" (7.5 to 12.5 cm). Secure hydrangeas and wild roses, one variety at a time, by applying hot glue to lower 1½" (3.8 cm) of stems.

4 Secure freesia to garland, as in step 3. Space the flowers evenly throughout the garland.

5 Apply glue to ends of the filler flowers, and insert them into the garland, one variety at a time, to fill in any bare areas. Insert twigs, vines, and ribbon, if desired.

HONEYSUCKLE GARLANDS

A decorative honeysuckle garland can adorn a table, wall, or mantel. Garlands can be filled with wisps of greenery or short, dense foliage, depending on the lengths of the floral materials used.

Garlands made of dried materials are fragile, and large garlands can be difficult to carry and arrange after they are finished. Therefore, you may want to construct the garland in the location where it will be displayed.

HOW TO MAKE A HONEYSUCKLE GARLAND

MATERIALS

- Honeysuckle vines.
- Preserved plumosa or other foliage.
- Silk and parchment roses or other dominant flowers.
- Dried pepper berries and nigella pods or other secondary materials.
- Dried pepper grass, statice, and veronica or other filler materials.
- Wire cutter.
- Paddle floral wire.
- Ribbon.

1 Cut the honeysuckle vines to arcs of desired lengths; secure together, using floral wire.

2 Insert sprigs of plumosa into vines until the desired fullness is achieved; secure with hot glue. Short stems make a more compact design.

3 Insert largest rose into center of garland to create a focal point. Insert remaining roses, spacing them evenly throughout garland; secure with hot glue.

4 Insert pepper berries so they radiate from central focal point; space evenly. Insert nigella pods, spacing evenly throughout.

5 Insert pepper grass, statice, and veronica, one variety at a time, radiating from the focal point. Insert ribbon into garland, forming loops at center; secure with hot glue.

IDEAS FOR CHRISTMAS GARLANDS

Garland is used traditionally to dress the mantel. To secure the garland without nailing into the mantel itself, cut a 1 × 1 board the length of the mantel. Stain or paint the board to match the mantel, and pound nails into the board for securing the garland.

Swag is draped high above a fireplace, and sprays are displayed on each side. To make a pair of sprays from an artificial garland, cut a 9-foot (2.75 meter) garland in half. Fold each piece in half, creating two sprays, and embellish them as desired.

Safety note: Do not leave any open flame, including candles, unattended. For fireplaces, always use a fire screen. (Screen was removed for photo effect.)

Bow-shaped garland is hung over the fireplace instead of a wreath. Tie a wide ribbon to the ends of the garland, and hang the garland from the ribbon.

Fresh garland is used to decorate a bannister. To protect wood surfaces, use chenille stems instead of wire when making the garland.

*Baskets,
Bundles
& More*

WALL BASKETS

Wall baskets can be filled with dried line and filler materials. Dominant and secondary flowers may also be added, if desired. You may want to embellish the arrangement with a ribbon or raffia bow.

HOW TO MAKE A WALL BASKET

MATERIALS

- Eucalyptus or other line material.
- Dried roses, strawflowers, globe amaranth, and nigella pods or other filler materials.
- Wall basket.
- Floral foam for dried arranging.
- Sheet moss.
- Wire cutter.
- 22-gauge paddle floral wire.

1 Line basket with moss, if necessary. Cut the foam to fit basket. Insert wire through foam, placing small twig between wire and foam; pull wire through foam to back side.

2 Insert foam into basket. Pull wire through back of basket; twist to secure. Cover foam with sheet moss; mist moss lightly with water.

3 Insert sprigs of eucalyptus into foam; fan out evenly.

4 Insert filler materials into arrangement, one variety at a time, spacing evenly.

Wall baskets with floral arrangements add interest to walls. Change the look throughout the year by selecting flowers that reflect the seasons. For long-lasting arrangements, select silk or parchment floral materials.

For arrangements with soft, subtle colors, use dried floral materials. A wide variety of silk, preserved, and dried floral materials is available at floral shops and craft stores.

For easy arrangements, choose two or three foliage materials to form a base for the flowers. Then choose flowers, in several sizes, that are appropriate for the season. Accent the arrangement, if desired, with items such as pinecones, pomegranates, ribbon or raffia bows, and small twigs.

Summer basket (opposite) displays several varieties of colorful floral materials.

Spring basket (above) features clustered lilacs and daffodils inserted into a base of ivy. Pussy willow stems, plumosa, and freesia are added for more texture.

Fall basket consists of several preserved foliage materials, accented with dried hydrangea and artichokes. Poppy pods, bittersweet, and curly willow stems provide additional interest.

Winter basket has a base of preserved juniper. Berry stems, dried pepper stems, pinecones, and pomegranates add visual interest. Curly willow stems are sprayed gold for a festive look.

daffodils

ivy

freesia

lilac

Spring

pussy willows

plumosa

curly willow

pomegranate

Winter

chili peppers

juniper

FLORAL MATERIALS FOR SEASONAL WALL BASKETS

Silk, parchment, and dried flowers and the foliage shown can be used to make seasonal arrangements. Consider varieties that grow locally; you may choose to gather fresh floral materials for drying (pages 82-85).

cone

berries

HOW TO MAKE A SEASONAL WALL BASKET

MATERIALS

- Wall basket.
- Floral foam for silk or dried arranging; serrated knife; brown craft paper.
- Sheet moss or Spanish moss.
- Silk, parchment, or dried foliage in one or more varieties.
- Silk, parchment, or dried flowers in various sizes.
- Embellishments, optional.
- Hot glue gun and glue sticks.
- Aerosol clear acrylic sealer, for dried arrangements.

1 Line interior of basket with crumpled paper, to cover any open areas of basket. Using the knife, cut foam to fit the basket, allowing ease; extend the foam about 2" (5 cm) above the basket. Cover foam with moss.

2 Insert first variety of foliage into the container; place the taller stems into the center near the back and the shorter stems at the sides and front, fanning the materials out evenly. Insert any remaining varieties of foliage or small filler flowers, one variety at a time, spacing them evenly.

sweet peas

asters

astilbe

irises

cosmos

Summer

Fall

oak leaves

bittersweet

artichoke

seeded
eucalyptus

hydrangea

twigs

poppy
pods

3 Insert
any large
flowers into
arrangement,
one variety
at a time,
spacing
them evenly
throughout
to keep the
arrangement
balanced on
three sides.

4 Insert any
medium-size
flowers into the
arrangement to
fill in any bare
areas. Insert
embellishments
as desired,
securing with
hot glue. Apply
aerosol clear
acrylic sealer
to dried floral
arrangements.

GARDEN BASKETS

Floor baskets containing potted florals bring a garden look into any interior. Use one as an accent near a fireplace or next to a favorite chair. This versatile basket arrangement also works well in a bedroom or entryway. It is made by placing three clay pots into a large basket, filling them with dried naturals, and surrounding them with moss.

HOW TO MAKE A GARDEN BASKET

MATERIALS

- Dried roses, larkspur, and oregano or other dried materials.
- Basket with handle, about 15" × 18" (38 × 46 cm).
- Three clay pots, about 6" (15 cm) in diameter.
- Floral foam for dried arranging.
- Spanish moss and sheet moss.
- Wire cutter; serrated knife.
- Hot glue gun and glue sticks.

1 Cut thin layer of foam to fit inside bottom of basket. Secure foam to basket, using hot glue. Cover bottoms of pots with hot glue, and press them into foam base, allowing pots to tip outward slightly, if desired.

2 Cut foam into pieces, and wedge into the area between pots and basket, keeping height of foam 2" (5 cm) below top edges of pots. Cover foam with sheet moss, securing it with hot glue. Also insert foam into clay pots, and cover with Spanish moss (page 23).

3 Insert one variety of dried natural into each pot, starting at center of pot and working out in a circle until the desired fullness is achieved. Stems in outer rows may be shorter than stems in center. Within a single variety, flowers may be positioned on each side of the handle. Fill in around edges of pots with additional Spanish moss, if desired.

SEASONAL ARRANGEMENTS

For a versatile floral arrangement that can be used as a centerpiece or atop an armoire, prepare a basketful of silk greenery, accenting it with flowers, berries, or dried naturals that reflect the season. Change the accents as the seasons change for a new look. For a fast and easy arrangement, select full clusters of silk greens with long, flexible stems that can be arranged for a natural appearance.

MATERIALS

- Basket or other desired container.
- Silk greens.
- Floral Styrofoam®.
- Floral adhesive clay.
- Spanish moss.
- Spring embellishments, such as silk irises and crocuses and pussy-willow stems.

- Summer embellishments, such as silk daisies, latex fruit, and branches.
- Fall embellishments, such as honeysuckle vines, preserved autumn leaves, and dried pods.
- Winter embellishments, such as artificial greens, pinecones, and assorted berries.

Spring arrangement *(opposite) features the fresh look of irises, crocuses, and pussy willows. Insert the flowers, clustering each variety and varying the height of the stems. For added texture, insert several pussy-willow stems, varying the height.*

Summer arrangement *(right) is a bright accent for a sunny room. Insert stems of daisies, varying the height of the stems. For added texture, insert latex fruit and several branches, varying the height.*

Autumn arrangement *(below, left) has the warm colors of the season. Tuck short lengths of honeysuckle vine among the greens. Insert several stems of bittersweet and autumn leaves.*

Winter arrangement *(below, right) uses seasonal embellishments that outlast the Christmas holiday. Insert artificial evergreens, pinecones, and assorted berries.*

HOW TO MAKE A SEASONAL ARRANGEMENT

1 Cut the floral Styrofoam to fit the basket snugly; top of foam should be slightly lower than top of basket. Secure the foam, if necessary, using floral adhesive clay. Cover the foam with Spanish moss.

2 Insert stems of greens into the foam. Shape individual stems into soft curves, bending ends of tendrils for natural appearance. Add seasonal embellishments.

151

FRUIT BASKETS

Fruit baskets are traditional arrangements that make excellent centerpieces in the dining room or kitchen. They are perfect arrangements for informal settings. Use seasonal elements, or pick up a color or theme that coordinates with the decorating scheme of a room. For easy arranging, purchase latex, plastic, or papier-mâché fruit on wire or wooden stems. Or add your own stems to artificial fruit, using stem wire or wooden picks (page 24).

HOW TO MAKE A FRUIT BASKET

MATERIALS

- Fruits such as apples, plums, pomegranates, grapes, pears, nectarines, and cherries on wire or wooden stems.
- Silk pumpkin vines or other leafy foliage.
- Basket.
- Floral Styrofoam® for silk arranging.

- Spanish moss, sheet moss, or a combination of both.
- 16-gauge floral wire and floral tape; or wooden picks and awl if fruit is not prewired.
- Wire cutter; serrated knife; floral pins.
- Hot glue gun and glue sticks.

1 Insert foam in basket (page 23). Cover foam with Spanish moss, sheet moss, or a combination of both; combine mosses to give a more textured and natural look.

2 Add picks or wire to fruit, if necessary (page 24). Separate fruit by variety and by color. Select color that dominates, such as purple, and insert largest items first, one variety at a time; allow grapes to drape over edges of basket. Set aside smallest purple items to insert later. Check the arrangement for balance after each variety is inserted.

3 Select second most dominant color, such as red, and insert fruit evenly throughout the basket, one variety at a time; set aside the smallest red items to insert later.

4 Repeat step 3 with remaining fruit, spacing evenly throughout. Check arrangement from all sides for balance.

5 Place the smallest items into basket to fill in bare areas and to balance color throughout arrangement. Insert pumpkin vine to fill in remaining bare areas and to soften design. Bend and shape stems to give a natural appearance.

Wire basket (above) combines apples, grapes, pinecones, and nuts in a festive display. Seeded eucalyptus is used as filler.

Ceramic urn (opposite) replaces the traditional basket for a classic fruit centerpiece. Grape clusters drape over the sides for a dramatic effect. Ivy is used as filler, and honeysuckle vines spiral throughout the arrangement.

Grapevine basket (right) combines summer fruits and melons. The berries are added for textural interest and color contrast.

HARVEST BASKETS

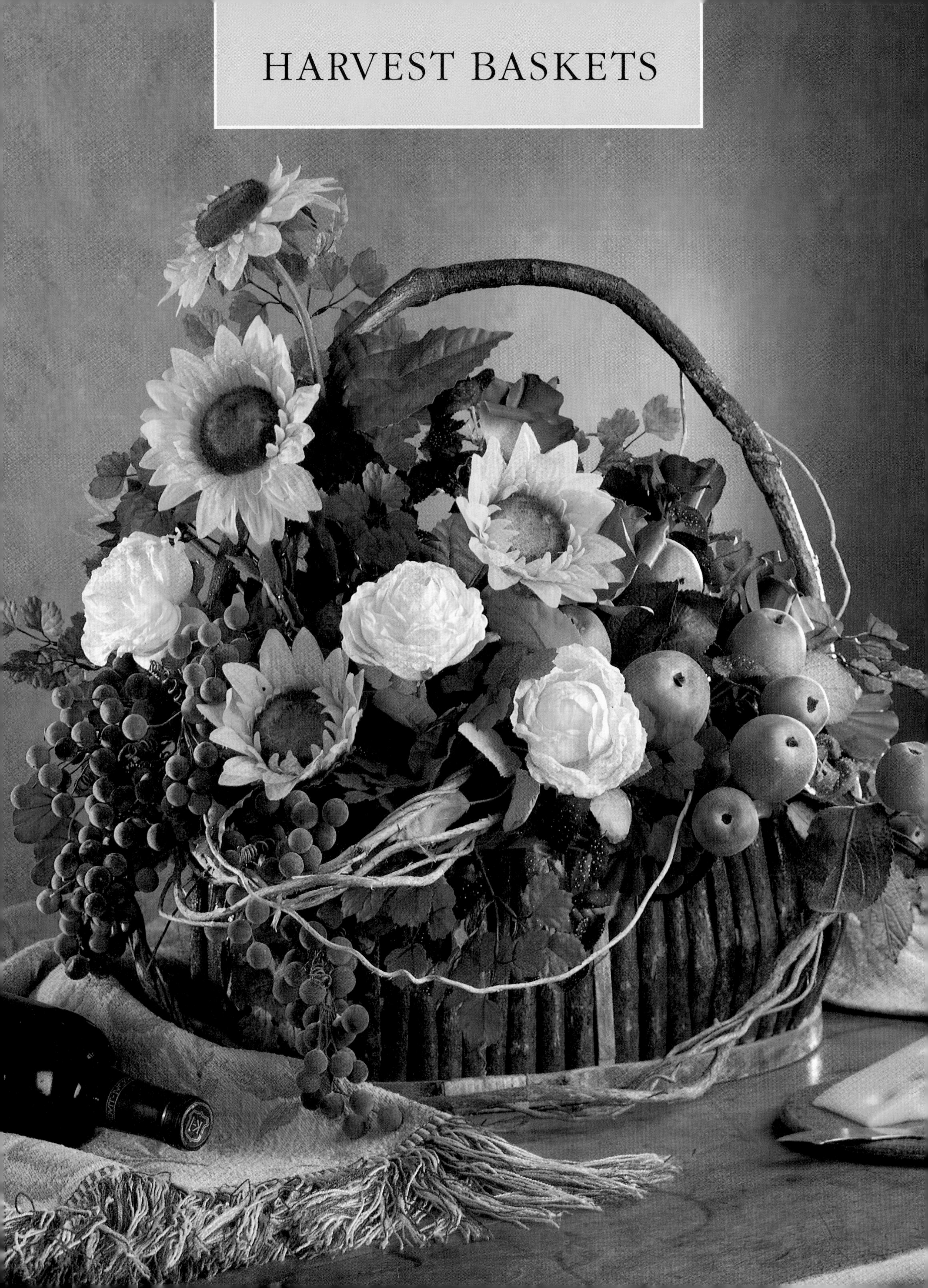

Harvest baskets, traditionally used in the autumn to gather nature's bounty, are re-created with silk flowers and latex fruit. A harvest basket complements any interior, from traditional to contemporary to country, mixing flowers and foliage with other desired elements.

Floral materials can easily be changed to reflect the current season or holiday. Place a traditional harvest basket on a fireplace hearth, or create a seasonal display for a kitchen or dining area.

MATERIALS

- Silk sunflowers or other dominant flowers.
- Silk roses and rosebuds or other secondary flowers.
- Silk begonia or other leafy plant.
- Silk autumn foliage and ginkgo or other filler materials.
- Two clusters of artificial apples or other large fruit measuring 1½" to 2½" (3.8 to 6.5 cm) in diameter.

- Five clusters of artificial grapes, to balance apples.
- Several 20" (51 cm) lengths of honeysuckle vine.
- Hickory bark basket with handle, about 12" × 15" (30.5 × 38 cm).
- Floral Styrofoam® for silk arranging.
- Spanish moss.
- Wire cutter; serrated knife; floral pins.

HOW TO MAKE A HARVEST BASKET

1 Insert foam in container, and cover (page 23). Wrap honeysuckle vines around basket, and insert ends into foam.

2 Cut sunflower stems with a wire cutter so flowers stair-step in height from top of basket handle to rim. Insert sunflowers on left side, with tallest stems to the left of center and shorter ones near the outside.

3 Add floral picks to fruit (page 24). Insert apples on right side toward front of basket, and insert central stem of begonia plant into center. Allow plant stems to cascade between other items.

4 Cut all rosebuds to the same height; insert them evenly on right side of arrangement. Bend and shape stems and leaves for a natural appearance.

5 Insert grape clusters on the left side, allowing them to cascade over front of basket. Cut rose stems, and insert in diagonal line on left side.

6 Cut foliage to desired lengths, and insert into bare areas of arrangement.

MORE IDEAS FOR HARVEST BASKETS

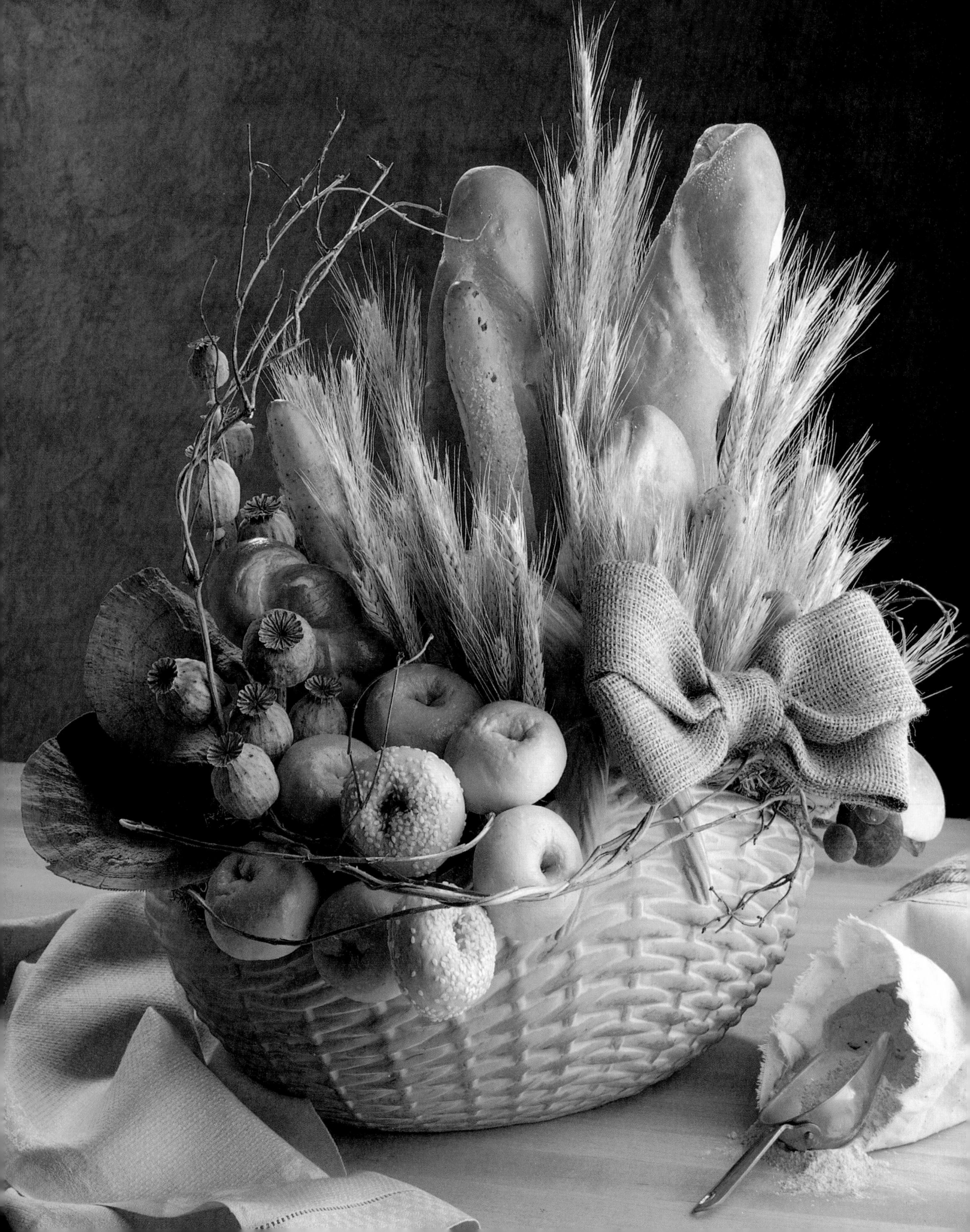

Holiday basket *features poinsettia as the dominant flowers, with artificial berries and chestnuts extending over the sides of the basket. A gold and green bow ties together the gilded walnuts (page 24) and the green sprigs of cedar and holly. Twigs are used as line material.*

Spring basket *has clustered spring flowers. A craft bird and several nests are used as accents. The artificial eggs are covered with flower petals as on page 219.*

Kitchen basket *(opposite) is filled with decorative breads, wheat, poppy pods, and mushrooms. The breads are coated with an aerosol acrylic sealer. Honeysuckle vines and a burlap bow are used as accents.*

Vegetable basket *(right) displays an array of garden vegetables. Vines of squash flowers twist around the basket handle. Pea pods are draped on the left, and squash hangs over the edge of the basket.*

WALL BUNDLES

Long-stemmed dried naturals, arranged for a bundled appearance, create an attractive wall accent. Ideal for filling a narrow wall space, wall bundles can also be grouped together for larger displays.

This arrangement works well using long-stemmed grains, grasses, or flowers. Choose a dried natural in a texture or color that blends with the decorating scheme. Then use a trim, such as paper twist, rope, raffia, or ribbon, for embellishing the bundle.

MATERIALS

- Dried naturals, such as barley, lavender, rye, roses, or delphinium.
- Decorative trim, such as paper twist, rope, raffia, or ribbon.
- Styrofoam®, 2" (5 cm) thick; serrated knife.
- Heavyweight corrugated paper.
- Cardboard; masking tape.
- 14" (35.5 cm) length of 18-gauge floral wire, for hanger.
- 22-gauge or 24-gauge paddle floral wire; wire cutter.
- Low-temperature glue gun and glue sticks.
- Embellishments, such as dried leaves and artificial berries or grape clusters.

HOW TO MAKE A WALL BUNDLE

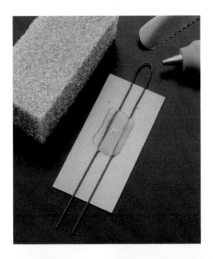

1 Cut Styrofoam to the desired width, using serrated knife; cut the height of the Styrofoam to about 4" (10 cm). Cut one 2" × 4" (5 × 10 cm) piece of cardboard. Bend floral wire in half, and glue it to cardboard, with looped end of wire extending about 1" (2.5 cm) beyond cardboard as shown.

2 Apply glue generously to the wire side of cardboard; center, and secure to back side of Styrofoam. Cut a 6" (15 cm) strip of corrugated paper to wrap around front and sides of Styrofoam and extend to back. Secure corrugated paper to Styrofoam with glue.

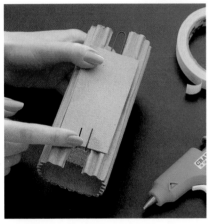

3 Glue a piece of cardboard, cut to same size as Styrofoam back, over back of base for reinforcement. Bend ends of wire around cardboard; cover the ends of wire with masking tape.

4 Glue a single layer of stems to corrugated paper, evenly covering the front and sides; center the stems lengthwise on base.

5 Layer additional stems over the previous layer. Wrap wire around base and stems; twist to secure, leaving slack for adjusting the placement of stems. Adjust placement of stems for even distribution and desired height.

6 Wrap second piece of wire around bundle, positioning the wire at the desired location for trim; secure tightly. Remove first wire. Apply glue along wire to prevent any slippage of the stems.

7 Trim ends of stems straight across or at an angle, using scissors. Tie or glue desired trim around bundle, concealing wire and glue. Secure embellishments to front of bundle with glue.

FLORAL BUNDLES

Long-stemmed dried naturals bundled in decorative containers make simple, attractive arrangements. Several bundles of various heights can be grouped for added impact.

For tall floral bundles, select a container that is heavy enough to support the height of the plant. If necessary, weight the bottom of the container with rocks or sand.

HOW TO MAKE A FLORAL BUNDLE

MATERIALS

• Dried naturals, such as roses, lavender, or rye.

• Decorative container.

• Floral arranging foam, such as by The John Henry Company.

• Sheet moss or Spanish moss; floral pins.

• 1½ yd. (1.4 m) ribbon or paper twist, optional.

1 Cut floral foam, using knife, so foam fits container snugly and is about ½" (1.3 cm) from top; cut and insert foam wedges as necessary. Cover foam with moss, securing it with floral pins.

2 Insert stems of dried naturals into foam, starting in center and working out in a circle until desired fullness is achieved. Stems in the outer rows may be shorter than in the center.

3 Wrap a ribbon or paper twist around the bundle, if desired; tie in a bow.

MORE IDEAS FOR FLORAL BUNDLES

Bundle of grain and flowers is arranged in a small, aged terra cotta pot. The bow is tied close to the pot, allowing the grain to flare gently.

Tiers of roses and cockscomb are simply arranged in a decorative pot.

Tiny dried roses are arranged in a small metal pot.

FLORAL BOUQUETS

Flowers may be gathered together to create a floral accent with a variety of uses. Floral bouquets may be hung on a door or bedpost, or be placed on a tabletop. They may be made from herbs to decorate the kitchen, from flowers to decorate a bedroom, or from evergreen branches to decorate a wreath or the foyer for the holidays.

HOW TO MAKE FLORAL BOUQUETS

MATERIALS

- Silk roses or other dominant flowers.
- Silk lilacs in two colors or other secondary flowers.
- Silk gingko or other foliage.
- Rubber band.
- Ribbon or raffia for bow.

1 Lay the foliage on a flat surface, fanning stems as shown, to create a base.

2 Place lilacs on top of foliage, in a fan shape. Insert the smallest roses; tuck them under the lilacs, next to foliage. Place largest roses on top of lilacs. Extend length of floral stems, if necessary (page 24).

3 Secure ends of stems together, using a rubber band. Cover the rubber band with raffia or ribbon. Trim ends of stems even, if desired.

GARDEN BOXES

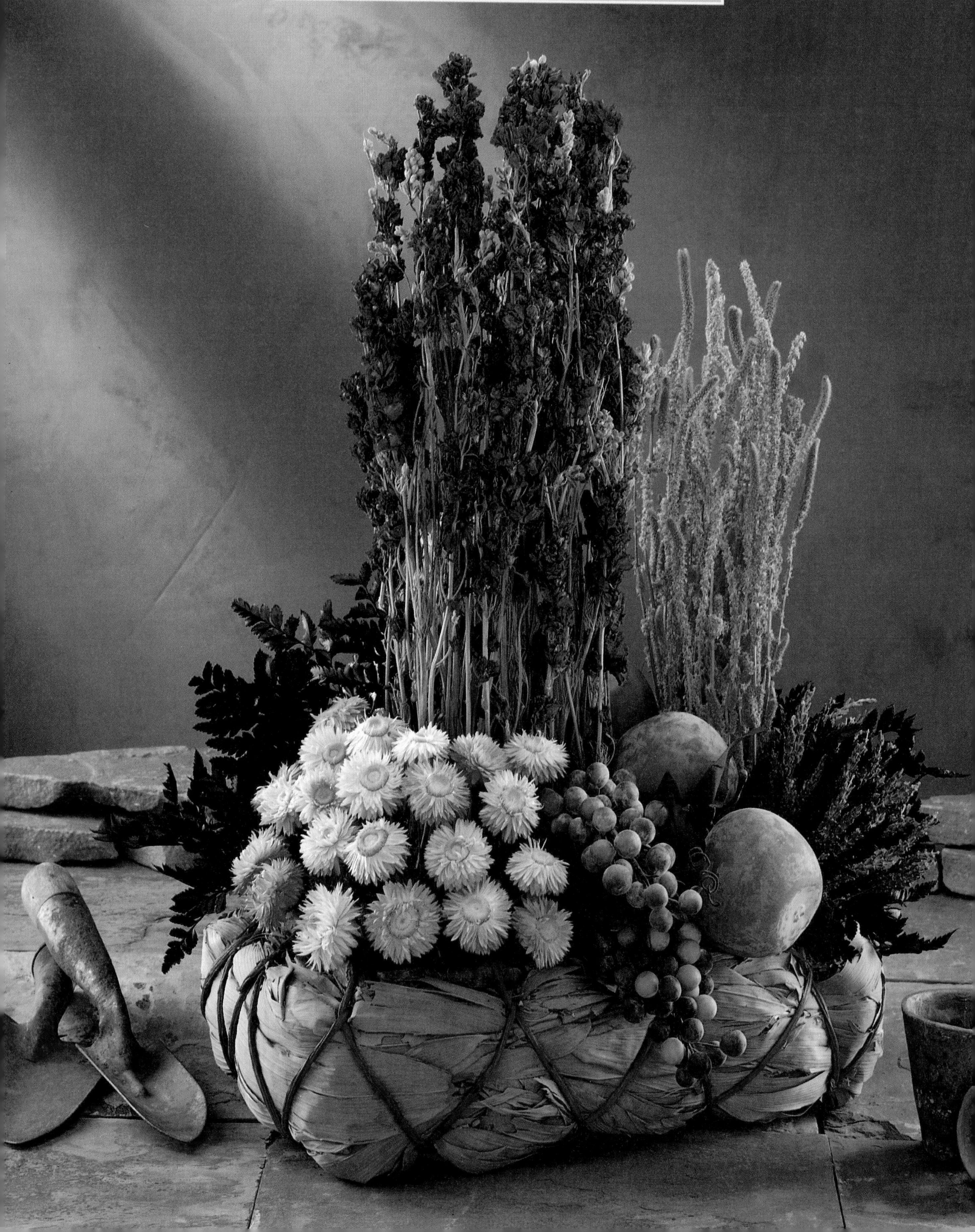

In European design, individual elements are grouped in separate areas instead of being mixed throughout the arrangement. European-style floral arrangements resembling miniature gardens fit well into casual living environments; a more formal look can be achieved by using decorative containers of brass or painted ceramic.

Fruits and berries can be interspersed among flowers for visual contrast. Garden boxes can be made with materials of varying heights, placing taller materials in the center or back of the container and shorter materials along the edges. Or use materials of uniform height arranged in geometric patterns, as on page 168.

HOW TO MAKE A GARDEN BOX OF VARYING HEIGHTS

MATERIALS

- Dried larkspur and limonium or other line materials.
- Dried strawflowers, globe amaranth, and lavender or other secondary flowers.
- Preserved leatherleaf or other dried foliage.
- Artificial fruits, such as apples and grapes, on wire or wooden stems.

- Rectangular container.
- Floral foam for dried arranging.
- Sheet moss.
- Wire cutter; serrated knife; scissors.
- Floral pins.

1 Insert floral foam into container, and cover with moss; secure with floral pins (page 23). Trim off excess moss with scissors, or tuck excess into sides of container.

2 Fill about one-third of container on left side with larkspur or tallest line material, staying 1½" (3.8 cm) away from edges. Insert limonium about 2" (5 cm) away from larkspur.

3 Insert wired apples (page 24) between the two line materials, near base. Place grape clusters in front of the larkspur, inserting one slightly higher than the other; allow them to cascade downward.

4 Insert the remaining flowers around line materials, clustering the flowers by variety. Place longer stems near the center and the shorter stems near the outer edges. Stems closest to the center point upward, and stems closer to the outer edges point outward.

5 Insert leatherleaf to fill in any bare areas; intersperse among flowers, if necessary.

HOW TO MAKE A GARDEN BOX OF UNIFORM HEIGHT

MATERIALS

- Dried materials such as miniature artichokes, nigella pods, cockscomb, pomegranates, poppy pods, strawflowers, and garlic bulbs.
- Rectangular container.
- Floral foam for dried arranging.
- Sheet moss.
- Wire cutter; serrated knife.
- String.
- Hot glue gun and glue sticks.

1 Insert foam into container, and cover (page 23). For dried materials with stems, cut the stems 1" to 1½" (2.5 to 3.8 cm) below flower head or pod.

2 Divide container into sections of equal size, using string. Apply hot glue to stems or underside of dried materials; insert a different variety into each section, keeping height of floral materials even.

MORE IDEAS FOR GARDEN BOXES

Thatched box *(left) combines lavender, roses, and rye in a parallel design, with equal space devoted to each. Floral materials rise 10" (25 cm) above the rim of the container.*

Shadow box *is filled with colorful flower heads, arranged in diagonal rows. The flowers are glued to a moss-covered sheet of foam board cut to fit in the shadow box.*

Wooden box *(right) contains grains, cattails, sunflowers, and poppy pods, arranged in vertical groupings. An array of dried and artificial fruits is inserted near the base.*

TOPIARIES

Topiaries are unique floral arrangements that can be used alone or in pairs for a classic look on a fireplace mantel or buffet table. The base of a topiary can be a candlestick, as shown here. Or it can be a branch or a wooden dowel set into plaster of Paris. At the top, a cone or ball is covered with moss, vines, and other floral embellishments. The cone or ball may be either a Styrofoam® or grapevine form.

Candlestick topiaries *are embellished with silk and dried floral materials for a romantic look.*

Moss topiaries *are displayed as a pair. The topiary on the left has two twigs intertwined to form the trunk. The topiary on the right is a simple variation, with the moss-covered sphere glued directly to the rim of the pot.*

Floor topiary *is embellished with honeysuckle vine, dried greens, and dried floral materials.*

Fruit topiary *is decorated with fruit slices, artificial fruit, and ribbon.*

Topiaries can be made from a candlestick and a Styrofoam® cone **(a).** Or for a topiary set in plaster of Paris, you can use a branch and a grapevine cone **(b)** or Styrofoam ball **(c).**

HOW TO MAKE A TOPIARY WITH A CANDLESTICK BASE

MATERIALS

- Silk roses, hydrangeas, and wild roses or other dominant flowers.
- Silk rose hips and astilbe and dried lepidium or other filler flowers.
- Artificial berries; huckleberry or other twigs.

- Silk ivy or other leafy plant.
- Candlestick; Styrofoam cone.
- Spanish moss.
- Wire cutter; floral adhesive clay; floral pins.
- Hot glue gun and glue sticks.

1 Place a ring of floral adhesive clay around the outer rim of candlestick. Apply hot glue generously over top of candlestick; allow glue to cool slightly. Center the base of Styrofoam cone over the candlestick. Press cone down into glue and floral adhesive clay, twisting slightly to secure.

2 Cover the cone lightly with Spanish moss; secure with floral pins. Cut ivy stems from plant, using a wire cutter. Insert stems into foam; wrap ivy tightly around the cone, securing with floral pins. Insert the stems of berries into cone, spacing them evenly.

3 Cut rose stems to lengths of 2" (5 cm); insert into cone, one variety at a time, spacing them evenly. Insert the hydrangeas throughout topiary, spacing evenly. Extend the length of hydrangea stems, if necessary (page 24).

4 Cut lepidium, rose hips, and astilbe to lengths ranging from 3" to 6" (7.5 to 15 cm); insert evenly throughout topiary, one variety at a time. Bend stems, and shape flowers and leaves as necessary to balance arrangement and to cover any bare areas. Embellish with twigs.

HOW TO MAKE A TOPIARY WITH A PLASTER OF PARIS BASE

MATERIALS

- Floral materials, such as moss, artificial fruits, and dried naturals.
- Wooden box, ceramic pot, or other desired container.
- Grapevine or Styrofoam® cone or ball.
- Branch, twigs, or dowel for trunk.

- Plaster of Paris; disposable container for mixing.
- Heavy-duty aluminum foil.
- Saw, floral wire, and wire cutter may be needed for some projects, depending on floral materials selected.
- Hot glue gun and glue sticks.

1 Grapevine form. Line container with two layers of aluminum foil. Crumple foil loosely to shape of container, to allow room for plaster to expand as it dries; edge of foil should be about ¾" (2 cm) below top of container.

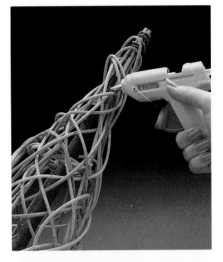

2 Insert trunk of tree into grapevine form as far as it will go. Place trunk in container, and adjust height of the topiary by cutting trunk to desired length. Secure grapevine form to trunk, using hot glue.

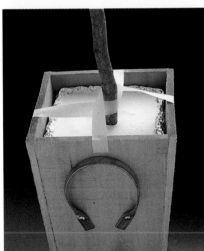

3 Mix the plaster of Paris, following manufacturer's instructions. Pour plaster into the container, filling to edge of foil. When plaster has started to thicken, insert trunk, making sure it stands straight. Support trunk, using tape as shown, until plaster has set.

4 Conceal plaster with moss or items that will be used to decorate topiary. Embellish grapevine form as desired.

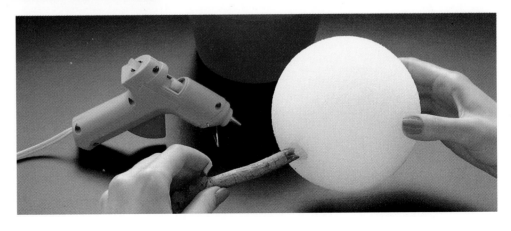

Styrofoam form. Prepare container as in step 1, above. Insert trunk of topiary into foam ball or cone to one-half the diameter of ball. Place trunk in the container, and adjust the height of topiary by cutting trunk to desired length. Apply hot glue into hole in foam ball; place ball on trunk. Continue as in steps 3 and 4, above.

Dyed pistachios *are used for casual topiaries that are inexpensive. On one small area at a time, apply hot glue to a painted Styrofoam® ball and quickly secure the pistachios with the unopened end down.*

Tiny dried rosebuds *are delicate and elegant for small topiaries. For easier insertion of the rosebud stems, make holes in the painted Styrofoam ball, using a toothpick, and dip the stems in craft glue before inserting them.*

Flowers and berries *have appealing color and texture. The selections for this topiary tree are hydrangea florets and pepper berries.*

Double topiary trees *are a variation of the basic tree. A ready-made topiary base, purchased at a floral shop, was used for this large floor tree. Pomegranates, oranges, and pinecones, secured with hot glue, are the primary embellishments.*

Sheer French ribbon *coils gently around the topiary tree opposite. Rosebuds and other embellishments are either secured with hot glue or inserted directly into the ball.*

CONE TREES

Cone trees are beautiful arrangements for buffet and side tables. After securing a Styrofoam® cone on an inverted basket, cover the cone with Spanish moss to provide a background for a wide variety of embellishments. Choose from dried naturals, cones, fresh or latex fruits, ribbons, and more. Use wooden picks (page 24) to insert fruits or to protect fragile dried selections; trim pick lengths as needed when working at the top of the tree.

HOW TO MAKE A DRIED-NATURAL CONE TREE

MATERIALS

- Styrofoam cone, about 18" (46 cm) high with 5" (12.5 cm) base.
- Woven basket with 5" (12.5 cm) base.
- Spanish moss.
- Preserved or artificial greens, such as spruce, cedar, and boxwood.
- 20 or more pinecones in various sizes.
- 11 yd. (10.1 m) ribbon, 3/8" (1 cm) wide.
- Several stems of small berries.
- Dried naturals, such as statice or baby's breath.
- 3" (7.5 cm) wooden floral picks with wire.
- Pruning shears; wire cutter.
- Craft glue; hot glue gun and glue sticks.

1 Apply hot glue to the top of the inverted basket; secure cone to basket. Arrange Spanish moss on cone, pulling moss apart so it loosely covers Styrofoam; secure with dots of hot glue, using glue sparingly.

2 Cut the greens into sprigs ranging from 3" to 6" (7.5 to 15 cm) long, making angled cuts. Insert the stems into cone, angling the sprigs so they point downward. Place longer sprigs at the bottom of the cone and shorter ones at the top; distribute evenly, but not in rows.

3 Cut the boxwood into pieces ranging from 3" to 6" (7.5 to 15 cm) long; intersperse other greens with boxwood.

4 Wire pinecones as on page 24. Insert pinecones, placing larger ones at the bottom and smaller ones at the top.

5 Cut berries into about 20 clusters; wire them to picks, and arrange on cone. Or attach stemmed clusters by inserting stems directly into cone.

6 Cut 15 to 20 clusters of statice; wire them to picks. Insert picks into cone, angling clusters so they point downward.

7 Cut ribbon into 1-yd. (0.95 m) lengths. Fold ribbon, forming three or four loops on each side; leave two tails, with one tail about 2" (5 cm) longer than the other. Attach to a wooden pick with wire, wrapping the wire around the center of the bow several times.

9 Attach bows to cone tree, inserting picks. Attach one bow to the top of the tree; shorten the pick on this bow, if necessary, and secure with glue.

8 Wrap longer tail of bow twice around center, concealing the wire; secure with the remaining wire, and twist wire around pick.

Floral
Accessories

DECORATING MANTELS

Family photographs *from previous Christmases are grouped on a mantel for a nostalgic holiday look. Honeysuckle vine and dried hydrangeas are used to embellish the artificial garland.*

Mantels are the perfect place to showcase special mementos and collections. Garlands arranged on a mantel can serve as a backdrop for a display of family photos or candlesticks. Tall or single-variety arrangements (pages 56 to 59) can emphasize favorite artwork displayed over the mantel.

Safety note: *Do not leave any open flame, including candles, unattended.*

Gilded reindeer
and candles in brass candlesticks (above) are arranged on an ornate mantel with greenery, cones, and berries. The papier-mâché reindeer were gilded with metallic paint.

Amaryllis *(right) are set on each side of a picture, dominating this winter display.*

Countdown calendar *(below) is made by hanging twenty-four stocking ornaments, filled with holiday candies, along a fresh garland. A star ornament hangs at the end of the garland for Christmas day.*

SEASONAL MANTELS

Mantels and fireplaces are ideal places for adding seasonal changes to your decorating. Arrangements can be changed easily without adding nail holes to walls, and since this area is often the focal point of a room, any changes have high impact.

Autumn arrangement (opposite) features a garland of twigs, preserved leaves, and bittersweet, draped over the mantel.

Make the garland by wiring clusters of twigs and leaves to a rope base. Secure the sprigs of bittersweet with hot glue.

Spring arrangement includes a collection of pots filled with silk tulips, crocuses, hyacinths, and Spanish moss. For interest, the height of the pots is varied. Wreath embellished with found objects is hung above the mantel.

Summer arrangement of tiered flowers fills the fireplace. A framed landscape and pots of silk foliage complete the look. The arrangement is simply made by inserting floral foam into a terra-cotta container, then inserting floral materials in rows, for a tiered display.

Winter arrangement with an evergreen garland base has clustered parchment flowers at the center. The arrangement is accented with pinecones, ornaments, and artificial-snow-covered sprigs of greenery.

FLORAL TOP TREATMENTS

Create a custom floral top treatment to complement simple window treatments or to embellish an otherwise bare window. The floral arrangement serves as a cornice, creating an elegant look. The arrangement is attached to a thin wood strip, covered with paper ribbon. For an arch window, cut a 2" to 3" (5 to 7.5 cm) wood strip to the shape of the arch from ¼" (6 mm) plywood.

The floral treatment may be attached to a curtain rod, using drapery hooks, or screwed into the wall at the sides of the window frame.

Design your own cornice, using moss, dried silk flowers, silk greens, twigs, and ribbons. Select elements that will complement the colors and atmosphere of the room.

Silk ivy is the dominant item used for this wall-mounted top treatment: twigs and two kinds of silk ferns are also used. A wood strip cut to the shape of the arch-top window is the base for the floral accent.

A variety of silk flowers is used for the rod-mounted top treatment shown at right. Silk greens, twigs, and wire ribbon are also strewn throughout the treatment.

Bundles of straw (opposite), bearded wheat, and other dried naturals are used for this wall-mounted treatment. Pheasant feathers and bittersweet berries are used as accents.

- 2" (5 cm) wood strip, such as pine lattice, cut to length of curtain rod, for rod-mounted treatment; or 2" to 3" (5 to 7.5 cm) strip of ¼" (6 mm) plywood, cut to shape of window, for wall-mounted treatment.

- Paper twist, untwisted.

- Hot glue gun and glue sticks.

- Moss; dried flowers, silk flowers, silk greens, twigs, and ribbon, as desired.

- Floral wire, for arranging heavier objects.

- Curtain rod and drapery hooks to fit over curtain rod, for rod-mounted treatment; or 8 × 1" (2.5 cm) pan-head screws and plastic anchors, for wall-mounted treatment.

- Drill; ³⁄₃₂" (2.38 mm) drill bit, for rod-mounted treatment; ⁵⁄₃₂" (3.8 mm) drill bit, for wall-mounted treatment.

HOW TO MAKE A FLORAL TOP TREATMENT (MOUNTED ON ROD)

1 Wrap board with paper twist, securing it with hot glue.

2 Predrill holes for drapery hooks; drill into edge of board, using ³⁄₃₂" (2.38 mm) drill bit and placing holes at 10" to 12" (25.5 to 30.5 cm) intervals.

3 Insert drapery hooks into drilled holes.

4 Secure layer of moss on front of board, if desired, using hot glue; moss conceals paper and provides background for design.

5 Arrange flowers, leaves, or other items as desired; for treatment shown here, start with background leaves, then add dominant flowers. Extend flowers, leaves, or other items beyond ends of board, for returns of curtain rod.

6 Complete the arrangement, filling in with additional leaves and flowers, as needed. Secure arranged flowers and leaves, using hot glue. Arrange ribbon as desired, forming loops; glue in place.

7 Hang cornice over curtain rod. For returns, attach moss to ends of curtain rod, using double-stick tape; glue or wire the flowers and leaves in place.

HOW TO MAKE A FLORAL TOP TREATMENT (MOUNTED ON WALL)

1 Follow step 1, opposite. Predrill holes for screws at ends and center of board, using ⁵⁄₃₂" (3.8 mm) drill bit; additional screws may be needed for wider windows.

2 Follow steps 4, 5, and 6, opposite; do not extend flowers and leaves beyond ends of board in step 5.

3 Screw plywood into wall next to window frame, using plastic anchors.

FRESH FRUIT CENTERPIECES

A cake stand is used as the base for this appealing table arrangement of fresh fruit, adding height and drama. A wide variety of fruits is used in the centerpiece, and, for even more visual interest, honeysuckle vines and fresh greenery are added.

MATERIALS

- Fresh fruit, including apples, pears, oranges, bananas, and grapes.
- Footed cake stand.
- Honeysuckle vines; fresh galax leaves.
- Filler materials, such as yarrow, ming fern, and salal leaves.

- Wired ribbon.
- Styrofoam® ball, 6" (15 cm) in diameter.
- Floral adhesive clay.
- Wooden skewers or picks; wired floral picks.

HOW TO MAKE A FRESH FRUIT CENTERPIECE

1 Cut Styrofoam ball in half; secure to top of cake stand with floral adhesive clay.

2 Insert honeysuckle vines into Styrofoam, allowing some vines to cascade around base of cake stand.

3 Insert wooden skewers or picks into apples 1" to 2" (2.5 to 5 cm). Secure to the Styrofoam, grouping apples closely on one side of the arrangement. Break off ends of skewers or picks if they are too long.

4 Secure pears on side opposite the apples, using wooden skewers or picks. Secure two clusters of oranges on opposite sides of the arrangement, between the apples and the pears.

5 Wrap wire from one floral pick around small cluster of bananas; insert floral pick into the Styrofoam, allowing bananas to cascade downward over the rim of cake stand. Repeat for cluster of bananas on the opposite side.

6 Wrap wire from one floral pick around two or three stems of fresh galax leaves; insert picks into the Styrofoam, filling in bare areas between clusters of fruit with leaves.

7 Wrap wire from one floral pick around clusters of grapes; space the grapes randomly, allowing some clusters to cascade over sides.

8 Fill in any remaining bare areas with filler materials, such as yarrow, ming fern, and salal leaves. Arrange a wired ribbon throughout the centerpiece, tucking ribbon into the crevices and draping it over the sides.

DRIED CORNUCOPIA CENTERPIECES

For an autumn feast, a cornucopia overflowing with dried naturals is a classic centerpiece. From the dozens of dried varieties available, select several, in a range of colors, shapes, and textures.

For a unique arrangement, consider using preserved roses, wheat, nigella pods, and yarrow instead of the more traditional gourds and Indian corn. For even more contrast in texture, accent the dried naturals with latex fruits.

To assemble the arrangement, fill the cornucopia with floral foam covered with moss. Then insert the dried naturals into the foam, one layer at a time.

MATERIALS

- Wicker cornucopia.
- Floral foam for dried arranging; sheet moss.
- Preserved autumn leaves; dried naturals, such as preserved roses, wheat, nigella pods, and yarrow.
- Latex or other artificial fruit, such as apples, grapes, and berries.
- 20-gauge floral wire; U-shaped floral pins; wired floral picks; hot glue gun and glue sticks.

HOW TO MAKE A DRIED CORNUCOPIA CENTERPIECE

1 Cut a piece of floral foam to fit inside cornucopia, using serrated knife. Insert wire through bottom of basket, then through foam.

2 Place a small piece of folded paper or cardboard on top of the foam, between wire ends; twist wire ends tightly over paper. This prevents wire from tearing the foam.

3 Cover foam loosely with moss; pin in place as necessary, using floral pins.

4 Insert the stems of the preserved leaves into the foam so leaves rest on table. Insert bunch of one type of dried naturals, such as nigella pods, into foam next to the leaves.

5 Insert cluster of latex grapes or other fruit on one side of the arrangement, above leaves. Wrap the wire from a floral pick around several stems of wheat; insert the pick into the foam near the center of arrangement, above leaves.

6 Insert several stems of roses in a cluster, next to grapes. Insert clusters of each remaining material, such as yarrow, arranging one variety at a time.

7 Fill in any bare areas with additional leaves or small grape clusters. Use hot glue, if necessary, to secure any individual items, such as single leaves, that cannot be inserted into foam.

MORE IDEAS FOR TABLE ARRANGEMENTS

Cuttings of ivy *are draped along the buffet table and interspersed among the serving pieces. Clusters of latex grapes are tucked in, next to the ivy.*

Hollowed-out fruits and vegetables *(below) are used in place of vases to display flowers.*

Assorted baskets (left) are grouped near the back of a buffet table. Arranged in the baskets are a variety of colorful fruits, vegetables, and breads.

CHRISTMAS TABLE ARRANGEMENTS

Wreath, *propped against the wall, provides a centerpiece for a side table and does not interfere with serving space. Position a cluster bow (page 108) at the top of the wreath, and add long tails to flow onto the table.*

Tinsel-filled ornaments, *clustered in a bowl and surrounded with greens, make a simple centerpiece. The ornaments are set aglow with miniature battery-operated lights.*

Fresh evergreen sprays, *placed end-to-end and topped with a bow, make a quick and attractive centerpiece. Candles are nestled in the greens.*

Artificial garland, *arranged in an S shape and embellished with golden artichokes and gilded pinecones and pomegranates, creates an easy and elegant centerpiece. This style is especially suited for long tables.*

HOW TO MAKE A FRESH EVERGREEN SPRAY CENTERPIECE

MATERIALS

- Fresh tips from various evergreens; cedar greens work well for the base.
- 22-gauge or 24-gauge wire; wire cutter; floral tape.
- Embellishments as desired, such as candles, ribbon, and berries.

1 Layer fresh greens, and secure stems with wire. Wrap wired stems with floral tape to protect the table, stretching the tape as it is applied. Repeat to make two garlands.

2 Overlap and wire stems of layered greens together; cover with floral tape.

3 Make bow with long tails (page 108), and secure to greens, concealing the wired stems. Twist and loop the streamers among the greens. Arrange candles and other embellishments as desired.

HOW TO MAKE AN ARTIFICIAL GARLAND CENTERPIECE

MATERIALS

- Artificial garland, 18" to 24" (46 to 61 cm) longer than desired length of centerpiece.
- French ribbon, about 18" (46 cm) longer than garland.
- Artichokes; dried pomegranates; pinecones; cinnamon sticks.
- Gold aerosol paint; gold wax-based paint.
- 26-gauge wire; wire cutter; floral tape.

1 Arrange garland in S shape on the table; adjust length, if necessary. Twist ribbon loosely throughout garland.

2 Apply gold aerosol paint to artichokes; spray the pinecones, if desired. Rub gold wax-based paint on pomegranates to add highlights. Wire pinecones and cinnamon sticks as on page 117.

3 Place artichokes near the center of the arrangement. Secure pinecones and cinnamon sticks to garland. Arrange the pomegranates between pinecones and cinnamon sticks. Arrange the candles as desired.

CANDLESTICK FLORAL ARRANGEMENTS

Fresh flowers, brass candlesticks, and tall tapers add grace and elegance to a formal table setting. Made from roses, star-of-Bethlehem, leatherleaf fern, caspia, and cornflowers, these candlestick arrangements are delicate and colorful. Different varieties of floral materials may be substituted, keeping the scale of the arrangement in mind.

MATERIALS

- Brass candlestick and taper candle.

- Roses; star-of-Bethlehem; leatherleaf fern; caspia; cornflowers.

- Floral foam cage, such as Oasis® Iglu™ holder for fresh flowers; plastic candle holder.

- Floral adhesive clay; 24-gauge floral wire; wire cutter.

HOW TO MAKE A CANDLESTICK FLORAL ARRANGEMENT

1 Apply floral adhesive clay to rim of the candlestick.

2 Soak floral foam cage in water until saturated; wire the cage to the top of candlestick, using 24-gauge floral wire.

3 Trim edges of plastic candle holder; insert candle holder into center of foam cage.

4 Cut the stems of the roses 1" to 1½" (2.5 to 3.8 cm) long, cutting diagonally under water with sharp knife. Insert stems into floral foam, spacing them evenly.

5 Cut star-of-Bethlehem stems 1" to 1½" (2.5 to 3.8 cm) long, cutting them diagonally with sharp knife. Insert stems into floral foam, spacing evenly. Allow some to drape downward.

7 Mist the arrangement with water; wipe the candlestick dry. Insert a candle.

6 Cut stems of leatherleaf fern, caspia, and cornflowers diagonally; insert into foam, filling any bare areas with fern and caspia and adding accents of cornflowers.

FLORAL TABLE ACCENTS

Serving tray *is embellished with a ring of silk ivy and flowers. The ivy vine encircles the platter, and the ends are twisted together. Stems of silk flowers are wrapped around the vine to embellish it.*

Votive candle *sits inside a hollowed-out dried artichoke that is sprayed with gold metallic paint.*

Coordinating arrangement and napkin accent *(opposite) make this breakfast tray festive. For the napkin accent, secure silk blossoms together with floral tape. French ribbon, tied around the napkin, conceals the tape.*

Goblet, place card holder, and napkin *(right) are embellished with dried flowers. The flowers are bundled together with floral tape and wrapped with ribbon. An additional ribbon secures the floral bundle to the goblet and the napkin. Hot glue holds the bundle to the place card holder.*

FLORAL ROOM ACCENTS

Chandelier *is decorated with floral corsages made of silk and dried floral materials. The arms of the chandelier are wrapped with ivy and raffia.*

Frame *with a flat surface is embellished with silk roses, dried hydrangea, and poppy pods.*

Basket *(left) with moss-covered rim is embellished with dried peonies, hydrangeas, carnations, pepper berries, and salal leaves.*

HOW TO ADD FLORAL ACCENTS TO A CHANDELIER

MATERIALS

- Floral materials as desired.
- Wire cutter; stem wire.
- Floral tape.
- Raffia or ribbon.

1 Add wire stems to individual floral materials, if necessary (page 24). Make raffia loops, and secure to wire stems. Combine materials into three small bunches; secure each bunch at top of stems, using floral tape.

2 Make floral corsage by securing the three floral bunches together 1" (2.5 cm) from top of stems, using floral tape.

3 Cut all but two stems from corsage. Bend and shape stems and leaves to achieve desired look. Secure the corsage to the chandelier, using the remaining stems.

HOW TO ADD FLORAL ACCENTS TO FRAMES & BASKETS

MATERIALS

- Floral materials as desired.
- Sheet moss.
- Frame or basket.
- Wire cutter; hot glue gun and glue sticks.

1 **Frame.** Cover frame with sheet moss, securing it with hot glue. Mist moss lightly, if desired, to make it more pliable.

2 Secure embellishments to frame as desired, using hot glue.

Basket. Cover the rim of the basket with sheet moss as in step 1. Secure embellishments to rim as desired, using hot glue.

PRESSED FLOWERS

Pressed flowers make beautiful accents for many home decorating accessories, including floral sun catchers, botanical artwork, and overdipped candles (pages 206 to 213). The pressed flowers are inexpensive to make, using flowers from your garden and a handmade flower press.

THE FLOWER PRESS

Although you have probably pressed flowers between the pages of a heavy book, a flower press will produce better results. The flower press consists of wooden front and back covers, with layers of corrugated cardboard between them. The flowers are pressed between the cardboard layers, with blotter paper or blank newsprint on both sides of the flowers. The blotter paper or newsprint absorbs the moisture from the flowers. The wing nuts on the corners of the press are tightened, to flatten the flowers as they dry.

FLOWER SELECTION

Flowers dried in a flower press usually retain much of their original color and take on a translucent quality. Select flowers that are in perfect condition, dry, and free of insects. Almost any flower can be preserved in a press, but some work better than others. Flat flowers and flowers with only a few petals, such as pansies and violas, can be pressed intact and, when pressed, will retain their natural form. However, to press flowers

with thick, hard centers, you must take the flowers apart, petal by petal, because of the difference in thickness between the flower parts. Then reassemble the flowers, gluing the petals together, when you use them in a project. The thick, hard centers must be pressed in a different layer of the flower press from the petals. Or discard the centers and substitute similar, but flatter, centers from another variety when reassembling the flowers.

Bell-shaped flowers, which are difficult to take apart, generally look better as three-dimensional, rather than pressed, flowers. Rose petals press well, but they cannot be reassembled into the original shape of the rose. Rosebuds can be sliced in half with a razor blade, and then pressed.

PRESSING THE FLOWERS

The flowers must remain in the press until they have lost all their moisture and feel papery. This usually takes one to two weeks, depending on the thickness of the flowers and the amount of moisture in the flowers at the time they were put into the flower press. Changing the sheets of blotter paper or the newsprint after several days speeds

the process and prevents the flowers from mildewing and browning; however, you risk damaging the flower when it is transferred to the fresh paper. To remove the flower from the press, either when changing the paper or when the flowers are completely dry, use tweezers with flat, rounded ends, such as those designed for stamp collecting. The sheets of blotter paper or newsprint can be reused after they have dried, provided they are not stained with mildew or dyes from the flowers.

Keep a log, listing the types of flowers that are being pressed in each layer, the dates they were put into the press, and the dates the blotter paper was changed. You may also want to include other information, such as where the flowers were gathered. By keeping a record, you will know exactly what is in the press without disturbing the materials before they are dry.

MATERIALS

- Two pieces of ½" (1.3 cm) plywood or medium-density fiberboard (MDF), each 9¾" × 12¼" (25 × 31.2 cm).
- Four ¼" × 3½" (6 mm × 9 cm) bolts with wing nuts and washers.
- Several sheets of corrugated cardboard with smooth, flat surfaces on both sides, each 9½" × 12" (24.3 × 30.5 cm).
- Several sheets of 19" × 24" (48.5 × 61 cm) blotter paper, each cut into four pieces that measure 9½" × 12" (24.3 × 30.5 cm); blank newsprint may be substituted, but do not use paper toweling or other textured papers that could imprint the flowers.
- Adhesive tabs, for numbering the cardboard layers.
- Mat knife; 220-grit sandpaper; drill and ¼" drill bit.
- Tweezers with flat, rounded ends, such as tweezers used by stamp collectors, for removing pressed flowers.
- Small notebook, for recording data.
- Plastic sleeves, wax paper, or wax paper envelopes used by stamp collectors, for storing the pressed flowers.

HOW TO MAKE A FLOWER PRESS

1 Measure ¾" (2 cm) from edges at each corner of wooden top cover; mark. Drill holes in the cover, using ¼" drill bit.

2 Use top cover as guide for marking position of holes in bottom cover. Drill holes in bottom cover. Sand all edges and surfaces of the covers.

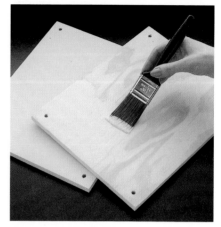

3 Stain or paint covers, if desired. Decorate the top cover, if desired, gluing dried floral materials or other embellishments in place.

4 Measure and mark the sides of the cardboard 2" (5 cm) from each corner. Using straightedge, draw a diagonal line across each corner, connecting the marks. Trim off each corner, using a mat knife.

5 Repeat step 4 for all pieces of cardboard and for the sheets of blotter paper or newsprint. Attach adhesive tabs to the edges of the cardboard pieces, labeling each of the layers consecutively.

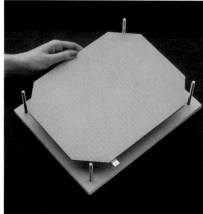

6 Assemble the press by putting the bolts through the back cover, from outside to inside. Lay the back cover on a flat surface, with inside facing up. Center the first sheet of cardboard over the cover.

7 Stack two sheets of blotter paper or four sheets of newsprint on top of the cardboard. Repeat the layers of cardboard and paper, ending with a piece of cardboard.

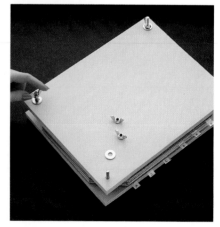

8 Insert the bolts through top cover. Place washers over the bolts, and secure with wing nuts.

HOW TO PRESS FLOWERS

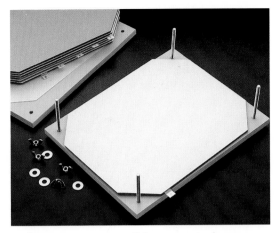

1 Remove top cover of the press, and remove all layers except the first piece of cardboard and one sheet of blotter paper or two sheets of newsprint.

2 Cut the stems close to flowers. Arrange the floral materials to be pressed on blotter paper or newsprint, allowing 1" (2.5 cm) of space around each item. Press materials of the same thickness on each layer.

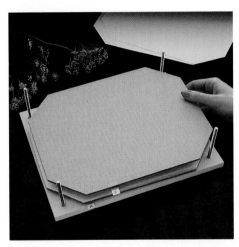

3 Cover with one sheet of blotter paper or two sheets of newsprint; then cover with one piece of cardboard.

4 Repeat steps 2 and 3 for any additional layers, sandwiching floral materials between the blotter paper or newsprint and separating each of the layers with cardboard. Keep a record of the items being pressed on each layer, along with the date they were put into the press and where they were gathered.

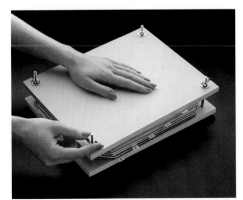

5 Insert bolts into corners of top cover; place a washer and a wing nut over the bolt at each corner. Secure the cover, tightening wing nuts as far as possible. Retighten wing nuts every day until they are fully tightened.

6 Check floral materials after one to two weeks to see if they are completely dry; take care not to disturb other layers. When dry, remove floral materials carefully, using tweezers, and store them flat in plastic sleeves, between layers of wax paper, or in wax paper envelopes. Label contents. Store the pressed flowers away from light and humidity.

FRAMED BOTANICALS

Pressed flowers and leaves can be mounted in prematted frames for a classic wall arrangement. The natural beauty of pressed flowers surpasses that of botanical prints, at a fraction of the cost.

Single large leaves or clusters of small pressed flowers and grasses can be arranged on rice paper for a textural background. Then cover the botanical materials with a sheet of extra-thin glass to hold them securely, and place the layers in a purchased frame.

MATERIALS

- Inexpensive frame with a precut mat.
- Extra-thin glass.
- Glass cutter.
- Rice paper.

- Pressed flowers, leaves, or grasses (page 202).
- Double-stick framer's tape or craft glue.
- Brads; split-joint pliers.

HOW TO MAKE FRAMED BOTANICALS

1 Remove the backing, precut mat, and glass from frame. Cut a piece of extra-thin glass as on page 211, cutting it to same size as the glass provided with the frame. Clean both of the glass pieces thoroughly.

2 Cut rice paper to fit the backing provided with frame. Attach paper to backing at corners, using double-stick framer's tape or dots of glue.

3 Arrange pressed floral materials on the rice paper, checking to see that arrangement fits within mat opening.

4 Position extra-thin glass over pressed floral materials and rice paper. Position precut mat over extra-thin glass.

5 Position the original glass over precut mat and other layers; then position the frame over the glass.

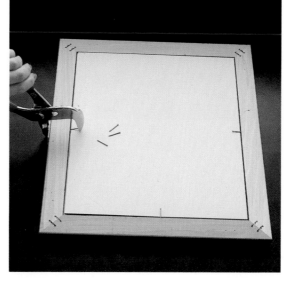

6 Turn frame over, keeping all layers firmly in place. Secure the layers into the frame, using small brads and split-joint pliers; pressure between layers keeps the flowers in place.

OVERDIPPED CANDLES

Pressed flowers and leaves can be applied to the surface of a candle and sealed with a light coating of wax, using a technique called *overdipping*. Plain candles can become one-of-a-kind candles that reflect your own garden or coordinate with a floral arrangement. The prepared candle is dipped through a shallow layer of melted wax floating on hot water. Because the water is not as hot as the wax, it does not affect the surface of the candle.

Melt the wax slowly on a stovetop or on a hot plate, using a double boiler. Or use a metal container set into a larger pan of water, with a metal rack placed in the water pan to raise the upper container. Use a candy thermometer to check the temperature of the melted wax. Dip candles with smooth movements, working quickly while the wax is hot. Avoid pouring any water that may contain melted wax into the sink, because wax solidifies quickly and will clog the drain.

HOW TO DECORATE AND OVERDIP A CANDLE

MATERIALS

- Candle in desired shape and size; for best results, the candle should be one color to its core, not an overdipped color.
- Pressed flowers (page 202) or other thin materials, for decorating the candle.
- Stainless steel spoon.
- Hot plate or stovetop burner.

- Soft work surface, such as a surface covered with several layers of fabric.
- Double boiler or alternative cans or saucepans.
- Paraffin wax.
- Freezer paper.
- Pliers; candy thermometer.

1 Place the bowl of a spoon over stovetop burner or hot plate, heated to low setting; or lean the bowl of a spoon against the soleplate of an iron at low setting. Arrange the pressed flowers or other thin materials as desired on the work surface to determine design you want to follow.

2 Transfer one of the larger background items to surface of the candle. Roll the heated bowl of the spoon over the surface of the item, working from center to outer edges and melting the wax under it; continue until all areas of the item are held in place by the rehardened wax. Reheat the spoon as needed.

3 Position and affix other items in the same manner, working with larger and background items first and filling in the spaces as desired with smaller items.

4 Place about ½ lb. (250 g) of wax in the top of a double boiler; place over a pan of hot water, and heat the wax to 205°F (96°C). Heat the water in a tall can to just below boiling; remove from heat. Slowly pour the wax onto surface of hot water, taking care not to cause bubbles to form in the wax. Remove any bubbles with a wooden spoon.

5 Hold candle by the wick with pliers. Dip candle up to wick; remove from dipping can. Allow to cool for a few seconds. Repeat the dipping process. Stand the candle on freezer paper to cool; or, if overdipping a candle that will not stand alone, clamp the wick securely and hang candle until cool.

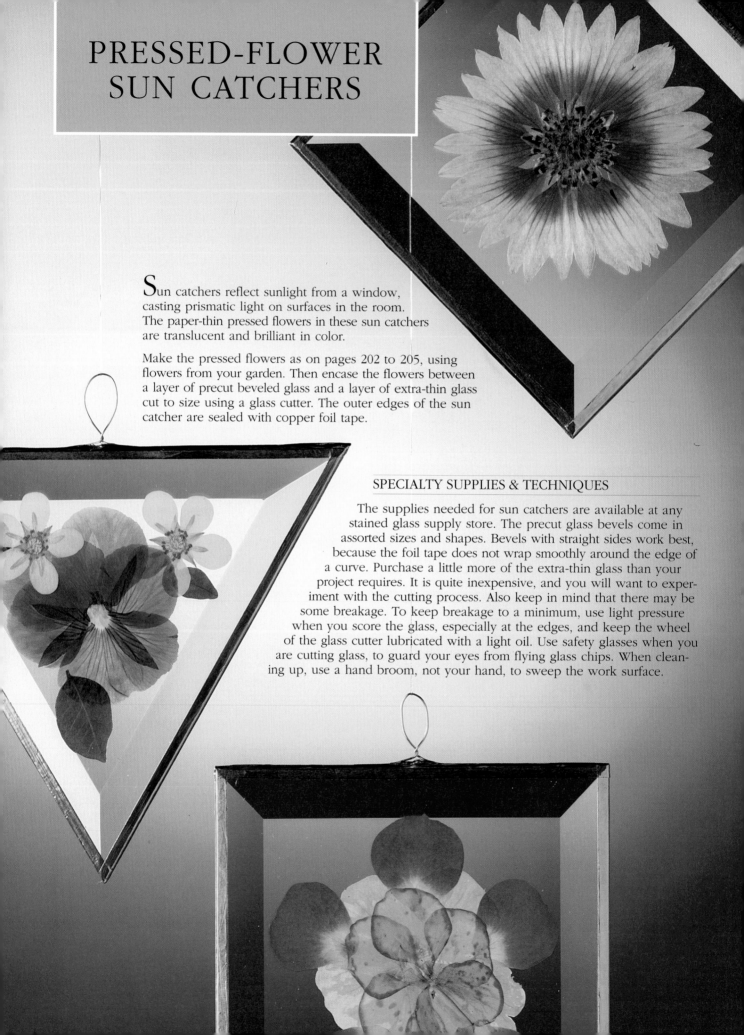

PRESSED-FLOWER SUN CATCHERS

Sun catchers reflect sunlight from a window, casting prismatic light on surfaces in the room. The paper-thin pressed flowers in these sun catchers are translucent and brilliant in color.

Make the pressed flowers as on pages 202 to 205, using flowers from your garden. Then encase the flowers between a layer of precut beveled glass and a layer of extra-thin glass cut to size using a glass cutter. The outer edges of the sun catcher are sealed with copper foil tape.

SPECIALTY SUPPLIES & TECHNIQUES

The supplies needed for sun catchers are available at any stained glass supply store. The precut glass bevels come in assorted sizes and shapes. Bevels with straight sides work best, because the foil tape does not wrap smoothly around the edge of a curve. Purchase a little more of the extra-thin glass than your project requires. It is quite inexpensive, and you will want to experiment with the cutting process. Also keep in mind that there may be some breakage. To keep breakage to a minimum, use light pressure when you score the glass, especially at the edges, and keep the wheel of the glass cutter lubricated with a light oil. Use safety glasses when you are cutting glass, to guard your eyes from flying glass chips. When cleaning up, use a hand broom, not your hand, to sweep the work surface.

- Beveled glass square, rectangle, or triangle in desired size.
- Pressed flowers, leaves, and grasses as desired.
- Extra-thin glass; glass cutter; grozing pliers.
- 24-gauge copper wire; ⅜" (1 cm) copper foil tape.
- Fine-tip marking pen; cork-backed straightedge; masking tape.

HOW TO CUT THE GLASS

1 Trace the shape of beveled glass piece onto extra-thin glass, using fine-tip marking pen. Use outer edges of the glass sheet as one or two sides whenever possible.

2 Place a straightedge along one marked line on the glass, from one edge of the glass sheet completely across to the opposite edge. Check to see that the wheel of the glass cutter (arrow) will line up exactly on the marked line.

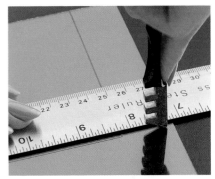

3 Hold the glass cutter perpendicular to the glass, with the wheel parallel to straightedge, beginning ⅛" (3 mm) from one edge of the glass. Hold the straightedge firmly in place with other hand.

4 Push or pull glass cutter, depending on which feels more comfortable for you, across the glass, from edge to edge, to score the glass; exert firm pressure, maintain a constant speed, and keep the glass cutter perpendicular to the glass. Ease up on the pressure as you score off the edges of the glass on the opposite side. Score the glass only once; do not repeat the process.

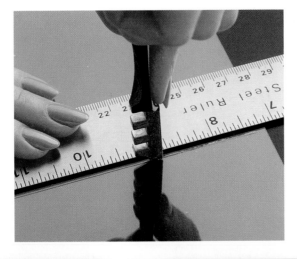

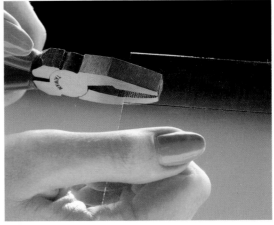

5 Hold the glass in both hands, with the scored line between your thumbs; curl your fingers under the glass, making fists, with knuckles touching each other.

6 Apply quick, even pressure as you roll your thumbs out from each other, turning your wrists upward; this breaks the glass along the scored line.

7 Repeat steps 2 to 6 for each of the remaining lines marked on the glass. For pieces that are too narrow to grasp with your fingers, use grozing pliers for safety and to obtain more leverage; hold the pliers at a right angle close to the end of the score and with flat jaw of the pliers on top of glass.

HOW TO MAKE A PRESSED-FLOWER SUN CATCHER
WITH A CORNER HANGER

1 Cut extra-thin glass (page 211) to the size of the beveled glass. Clean both surfaces of the beveled glass and the extra-thin glass piece with glass cleaner and lint-free cloth or paper towel.

2 Cut a length of the foil tape to the exact measurement of each side of beveled glass.

3 Place extra-thin glass piece facedown on clean surface. Arrange pressed flowers and leaves on center of glass in an area not larger than the center portion of beveled glass; materials under the bevel would appear distorted.

4 Place beveled glass, flat side down, over the pressed flowers, aligning glass edges. Adjust flower placement, if necessary.

5 Apply small pieces of masking tape to all sides of the sun catcher to hold it firmly together, keeping the flowers in place.

6 Decide which corner will contain hanger. Make hanger by forming a loop in copper wire, and cut the wire ends so they extend at least halfway down each adjacent side.

7 Peel paper backing from the strip of foil tape for lower edge of sun catcher. Holding the layered pieces of glass firmly in one hand, apply the foil tape to lower edge, centering tape on outer edge of glass so equal amounts will wrap to front and back.

8 Fold the foil tape to the front and back, smoothing it in place.

9 Apply foil tape to any remaining sides of the sun catcher that will not contain the hanger wire.

10 Apply tape to the sides adjacent to upper corner of sun catcher, centering the hanger wire along the edges of the glass and encasing it under the strips of foil tape.

11 Smooth all sides of the foil tape firmly, using handle of wooden spoon or wooden craft stick to ease out any bubbles or gaps.

12 Suspend sun catcher in a window, using fine nylon thread. For greater impact, arrange several sun catchers in one window.

HOW TO MAKE A PRESSED-FLOWER SUN CATCHER
WITH THE HANGER CENTERED ON ONE SIDE

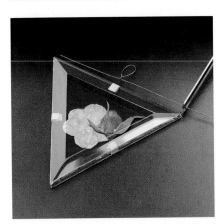

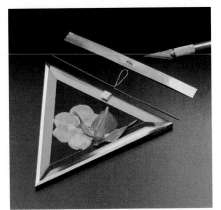

1 Follow steps 1 to 5, opposite. Decide which side will contain hanger. Make hanger by forming a loop in copper wire, and cut the wire ends so they extend to outer corners of the side.

2 Follow steps 7 to 9, opposite. Before removing paper backing from foil tape for upper side of sun catcher, cut small slit in center of foil tape, just large enough to insert the loop of the hanger.

3 Apply the tape to the upper side, centering wire along the edge of glass and encasing it under the tape. Complete sun catcher as in steps 11 and 12, above.

DECORATIVE CONTAINERS

A basket, box, or vase can be decorated with moss, leaves, or other floral materials to create a unique container for an arrangement. The base for the container may be made from a cardboard or wooden box, a glass vase, or a terra-cotta pot. The decorative containers may be embellished with a raffia or ribbon bow.

MATERIALS

- Basket, box, vase, or terra-cotta pot.
- Silk or preserved leaves, moss, pinecones, or flowers.
- Hot glue gun and glue sticks, or thick white craft glue.
- Raffia or ribbon, optional.

HOW TO MAKE DECORATIVE CONTAINERS

Leaves. Secure silk or preserved leaves in rows to vase or other container, using hot glue; overlap leaves as necessary to cover container. Leaves may be wrapped over the rim of the container, if desired. Embellish the container with raffia or ribbon as desired.

Pinecones. Cover cardboard box lightly with sheet moss; secure with hot glue. Cut the scales from one side of the pinecones, to make flat surface. Using hot glue, secure pinecones to sides of box with all pinecones facing in the same direction.

Moss. Secure sheet moss to sides of terra-cotta pot, using hot glue; cover the pot completely, and allow moss to extend slightly above the rim of the container.

Flowers. Secure flower petals to container, using thick white craft glue. For added embellishment, apply glue to the underside of flower heads and leaves; secure to the sides of the container.

DECORATING WIRE FORMS

Wire forms in various shapes and sizes can be covered with sheet moss for the look of a professionally groomed garden topiary. The forms, available from garden centers, craft stores, and mail-order suppliers, are first wrapped with wire mesh, then with the sheet moss, as shown below.

Other wire forms, such as bird cages, can be embellished with ivy vines, flowers, berries, and ribbons, using your creativity. Simply twist the vines around the wire forms, and use a hot glue gun to secure other embellishments.

HOW TO DECORATE WIRE FORMS

MATERIALS

- Wire form in desired shape, such as animal form.
- Wire mesh, such as chicken wire.
- Sheet moss.
- Wire cutter; paddle floral wire.

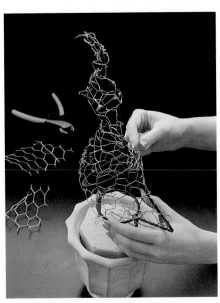

1 Place wire mesh over wire form, folding it around wire contours. Clip away any excess mesh, using a wire cutter; wrap wire ends around form as necessary to secure.

2 Mist the sheet moss lightly with water to make it more pliable. Cover wire form with sheet moss, securing it with floral wire.

Wire forms can be covered with sheet moss, as shown on the animal forms. Or accent wire forms like the bird cage and sphere topiary with vines, flowers, and foliage.

POMANDERS

Pomanders made from fragrant floral materials add a delicate aroma to a room. Hang pomanders decoratively in the center of a window or doorway. Or group them together to fill a bowl or basket, perhaps for a centerpiece on the dining-room table.

Fruit pomanders are created by shaping foam eggs and balls to resemble fruit shapes. Decorate them with flowers, petals, and leaves.

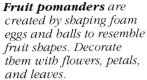

Pomander is covered with rose petals. Rosebuds, plumosa, and ribbons, secured with hot glue, add a finishing touch to the top of the pomander. The pomander may be tied to a lamp pull or bedpost.

Leaf-covered spheres are decorated with leaves. The leaves may be secured with glue, or secure them with brads for a decorative accent. Combine spheres of different sizes and types, grouping them together in a basket.

HOW TO MAKE FRUIT POMANDERS

MATERIALS

- Lavender, boxwood leaves, yarrow, rose petals, sunflower petals, globe amaranth, marigold petals or other desired floral materials.

- Dried or silk leaves, such as lemon verbena, pineapple, and grape.

- Twigs; cloves.

- Styrofoam® balls, eggs, and wreaths of various sizes, depending on the kinds and sizes of fruit desired.

- Wire cutter; serrated knife.

- Low-temperature glue gun and glue sticks; thick white craft glue.

1 Grapes. Apply white glue to small foam balls; roll the balls in lavender blossoms to cover. Allow to dry.

2 Form a grape cluster by securing several lavender-covered balls to 3" to 4" (7.5 to 10 cm) twig, using glue gun. Secure silk or dried leaf to end.

1 Pear. Press end of foam egg against table; roll gently from side to side to form shape for end of pear. Smooth the shape by pressing foam with fingers as necessary.

2 Apply white glue to foam; roll pear in boxwood leaves or yarrow to cover. Insert 2" (5 cm) twig into end of pear; secure, using glue gun.

1 Apple. Press a foam ball against table; roll lower two-thirds of ball gently from side to side to flatten and narrow slightly for bottom of apple.

2 Insert knife into top of apple at an angle; cut out a small cone shape about ½" (1.3 cm) long. Repeat at bottom of apple, cutting out a cone shape about ¼" (6 mm) long.

3 Smooth sharp edges by pressing foam with fingers. Apply white glue to foam, and roll in rose petals to cover. Insert 2" (5 cm) twig and lemon verbena leaves into top of apple; secure, using glue gun.

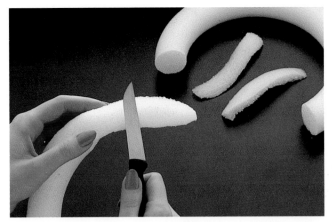

1 **Banana.** Cut 10" (25.5 cm) arc from Styrofoam wreath form; shape banana by trimming ends to points.

2 Apply white glue to foam; roll in sunflower petals to cover. Insert cloves into ends.

Pineapple. Trim lower end of foam egg to form flat base. Glue a stick into bottom of egg to make decorating easier. Apply glue to globe amaranth, using glue gun; insert pineapple leaves into top, securing with glue gun. Trim stick from base.

Orange. Make indentation in top and bottom of foam ball, using finger. Apply white glue to foam; roll in marigold petals to cover. Insert clove at each end.

HOW TO MAKE LEAF-COVERED POMANDERS

MATERIALS

- Styrofoam balls.
- Preserved, artificial, or fresh leaves.
- Low-temperature glue gun and glue sticks, or decorative brads.

Spheres with leaves. Secure leaves in rows to foam balls, using glue; each row overlaps leaves of previous row.

Spheres with leaves and brads. Secure leaves in rows to foam balls, inserting decorative brad at tip of each leaf to secure; each row overlaps leaves of previous row.

INDEX

Creative Publishing international, Inc.
offers a variety of how-to books. For
information write:
    Creative Publishing international, Inc.
    Subscriber Books
    5900 Green Oak Drive
    Minnetonka, MN 55343